Theme Park Insider
2016 Year in Review

Robert Niles

Copyright © 2016 Robert Niles

Published by Niles Online, 315 S. Sierra Madre Blvd., Pasadena, California 91107

All rights reserved. No part of this book may be reproduced in any manner without written permission except in the case of brief quotations embodied in critical articles and reviews. For more information, contact Niles Online, 315 S. Sierra Madre Blvd., Pasadena, CA 91107.

Theme Park Insider® is a registered trademark of Robert Niles.

Walt Disney World® and the names of its associated attractions are trademarks of the Walt Disney Company. Universal Orlando® and the names of its associated attractions are trademarks of NBCUniversal or its licensors. HARRY POTTER, characters, names and related indicia are trademarks of and © Warner Bros. Entertainment Inc. Harry Potter Publishing Rights © JKR. SeaWorld®, Busch Gardens® and the names of their associated attractions are trademarks of SeaWorld Parks & Resorts or its licensors. Neither this book nor ThemeParkInsider.com are in any way affiliated with nor endorsed by any of the parks or attractions listed within.

ISBN: 978-0-9909948-4-8

ACKNOWLEDGEMENTS

The author would like to thank the thousands of Theme Park Insider community members whose input helped inform the reader ratings and advice contained in this book. Special thanks also go to our front-page contributors, including Andy Farr, Douglas Hindley, AJ Hummel, Renata Primavera, and Bryan Schreier, as well as to all community members whose comments were included in the book.

CONTENTS

	Introduction	vii
1	Shanghai Disneyland Opens	1
2	Orlando and the Terrible, Horrible, No-Good, Very Bad Summer	18
3	Timing Is Everything: Theme Parks Move to Date-Specific Pricing	39
4	Disney Makes its Move with Marvel	50
5	Virtual Reality in the Parks	71
6	A Wizard Moves West: Universal Brings Harry Potter to Hollywood	86
7	Dubai Enters the Theme Park Business	99
8	The Rest of the Stories	116
9	The Best of 2016	128
10	A Look Toward 2017	142

INTRODUCTION

My first memory of a theme park is leaving one.

I must have been about two years old, slung across my grandfather's shoulder as he walked through the Disneyland parking lot at the of the day. The monorail had just rushed overhead, which must have awakened me.

I remember that sudden burst of excitement as I picked my head up from his shoulder and looked around. No, being at Disneyland wasn't a dream. I was still there! Of course, we were on our way back to the car after a long day in the park, so I wasn't going to be there much longer. But I remember to this day how happy I was at that moment, looking back at my first conscious day at Disneyland.

For more than 15 years, I've been helping people share memories of their theme park visits, on my website ThemeParkInsider.com. The site covers the world's most popular theme parks, reviewing new attractions, reporting on upcoming developments, and providing a forum for theme park fans to rate, review, plan, and discuss their visits to the parks.

This year, we are expanding our coverage to provide this book — a look back at the top stories, events, and attractions of 2016. In this "Year in Review," we will revisit seven of the most important and enduring stories that affected the theme park industry and its fans over the past 12 months. We'll then take a look back at a few of the other top posts that attracted the most attention on ThemeParkInsider.com this year.

We also will review the "Class of 2016," this year's new attractions at the world's top parks, honoring the best additions of the year and letting you know which rides, shows, and restaurants our readers rated as the "Must Do" attractions on your next visit to the Walt Disney World, Disneyland, and Universal Orlando resorts.

Finally, we will take a look ahead to 2017 and preview some of the newly announced attractions that will debut at the world's top parks next year.

Theme parks began 2016 with optimism. Attendance at the world's theme parks had grown by 7% in 2015, according to annual TEA/AECOM 2015 Theme Index, the industry's leading annual report on theme park attendance. With Disney opening its 12th theme park worldwide and offering new attractions on both coasts back in the United States, the industry's leader was expecting the strong attendance to continue in 2016. Disney's competitors at Universal, Six Flags, and Cedar Fair all had impressive new attractions in the works to debut this year, too.

But 2016 turned out differently in many markets. The nation's deadliest shooting and a horrific alligator attack shocked the Orlando community, leading the local theme parks to cancel or postpone media events and publicity campaigns to promote their new attractions. Other highly anticipated new rides and shows missed their deadlines. As the summer wrapped up, a hurricane struck Central Florida and closed the Orlando-area parks for the first time in more than a decade.

So as 2016 ends, we look back with a complicated mix of sadness, and even relief, along with the excitement and anticipation that typically accompanies the approach of a new year. We went through a lot in 2016.

But it sure made for one hell of a story.

SHANGHAI DISNEYLAND OPENS

On June 16, 2016, the Walt Disney Company opened its 12th theme park — Shanghai Disneyland. Disney's second theme park in China (after Hong Kong Disneyland) joined that park and the Disney resorts in Tokyo and Paris as the company's fourth theme park resort outside the United States. Shanghai might be the most unique among the world's Disneylands, however, with Disney's largest castle, an 11-acre "Gardens of Inspiration" replacing the traditional hub, and a unique line-up of "E"-ticket attractions, including an entirely new version of Pirates of the Caribbean, inspired by the Johnny Depp films.

Shanghai Disneyland also was wildly expensive to build, even though Disney owned only 43 percent of the project, with the rest held by the Chinese government through a holding company. Estimated construction costs swelled from around US$4 billion to more than $5.5 billion. The park also missed its initial planning opening at the end of 2015, leading to the loss of six months' income before its eventual opening in June 2016.

When theme park managers in the United States started blaming the Shanghai project for cuts in their own departments, Disney fans launched a sarcastic social media campaign with the hashtag #ThanksShanghai. But many fans set aside whatever ill will they might have felt about the project when the first on-ride video of the new Pirates ride and the TRON Lightcycle Power Run roller coaster hit the Internet. By almost all accounts, Shanghai Disneyland has been a creative success for the company, with the Pirates of the Caribbean Battle for the Sunken Treasure ride winning our Theme Park Insider Award for the world's Best New Attraction of 2016.

Whether Shanghai will be a financial success remains to be seen. Despite an initial rush of fans, crowds at the park have seem relatively sparse, as reports of lower than expected attendance have dogged the park in the months since its debut.

Don't Blame Shanghai for Cuts at Disneyland and Disney World
First published April 3, 2016

Over the past week, Disney fans have been Tweeting with the hashtag #ThanksShanghai — a sarcastic shout-out to Disney's newest theme park, whose cost overruns the fans blame for cutbacks at Disney's American theme parks.

Shanghai Disneyland opens on June 16, but Disney's target for the park was late last year. The delay has inflated the price of construction and has cost Disney its share of six months of income from what might end up becoming the world's most popular theme park. At the same time, fans are seeing cuts at the Walt Disney World and Disneyland Resorts, with fewer entertainment options, reduced capacity at some attractions, and reports of cast members seeing reductions in their hours scheduled.

It's easy to put two and two together, and... #ThanksShanghai. But blaming Shanghai Disneyland for operational cuts at Disneyland and Disney World reflects a simplistic conclusion. This just isn't the way that publicly-traded companies run.

To start, one basic rule of accounting is that capital expenditures — money spent on construction, new equipment, and buying land — is accounted differently that money for operations — such as paying employees. If Disney had to pay more than it planned to build Shanghai Disneyland, that's a hit to its capital budget. And no amount of cutting its operational budget will change that.

If Disney wants to offset an unexpected expense in its capital budget, it would need to do that by delaying or canceling another construction project. Now, there's a strong consensus within the analyst community that Disney already did that... by delaying Star Wars Land for nearly two years. Yes, the company was waiting for the start of the new trilogy, and yes, the company's board sent the original plans back to Imagineering for another go. It's possible, even likely, that Disney would have ended up delaying Star Wars Land even if it had never started the project in Shanghai. But it was a lot easier for Disney management to justify those capital delays when Shanghai was running over budget.

So what about that loss of six months' income? That *is* an operational issue. But in accounting terms, that delay was a one-time, extraordinary event. One-time items are the "get of of jail free" cards that companies hand to analysts, hoping not to be punished for a loss that doesn't reflect an ongoing problem in the company. Disney doesn't have to make cuts to balance that — analysts know what's up.

Of course, all of Disney's capital and operational expenses get thrown together on the company's bottom line. And any corporate executive who wants to keep her or his job wants that bottom line to look as black and as fat as possible. But any analyst with the ability to read a spreadsheet looks far beyond the bottom line. They know exactly what's happening in Shanghai. Nothing that Disney does stateside will hide that.

But... aren't cast members hearing from their managers that they're under orders to cut costs due to Shanghai? Here's where the corporate game of telephone comes into play. Of course, Disney wants to deliver the best bottom-line performance that it can, despite a hit from delays in Shanghai. So that's why upper-level executives would tell their department managers to take a hard look at all aspects of their operations, to see what might be cut to improve their departments' contributions to the bottom line. And yet... executives tell managers to get out the scissors all the time. With Bob Chapek taking over the Parks division from Tom Staggs last year, it's likely that such a call would have come anyway, with or without Shanghai in play. An immediate boost to the bottom line is an immediate boost to a new leader's reputation.

Disney always cuts labor hours in the shoulder season between Spring Break and the start of summer. And with Star Wars Land construction taking over large sections of Disneyland and Disney's Hollywood Studios, several attractions were going to close — whether for a short time or forever. But managers now are looking for whatever other cuts they can make to their labor and operational budgets, to see which ones they can "get away with," without resulting in a loss of income or attendance.

Many fans are citing the elimination of the Pixar Play Parade at Disney California Adventure for the next month as an example of #ThanksShanghai. But the festival marketplace food booths for the DCA Food & Wine Festival effectively block the park's parade route, making the parade impossible to run during the festival. Sure, Disney could have found other locations in the park for the booths, allowing both the parade and the festival to run at the same time. But here's how that cost-cutting analysis comes into play — Disneyland management is betting that it doesn't need the parade to draw visitors while the festival is running. And if the parade isn't going to improve the bottom line during the festival, why run it? Why not save the expense and let that flow to the bottom line?

Here's how you know that the current cuts at Disneyland and Disney World ultimately don't have anything to do with Shanghai. Imagine if Shanghai Disneyland becomes a wild financial success, earning more than Disney anticipated and contributing billions to the company's profit. What happens then?

Here's what happens — If the cuts at Disneyland and Disney World do not result in a loss of income or attendance at those parks, Disney won't change a thing. Disney will bank the extra profits from Shanghai and the extra profits from cutting superfluous expenses at DLR and WDW. The only way that Disney will back off cuts at its U.S. resorts will be if those cuts result in losses for the company. Ultimately, the parks' direction is not determined by what's happening in China. It will be determined by the decisions of Disney's theme park customers.

If fans decide that they'd rather go spend their money at Universal, Knott's, SeaWorld, Six Flags, or other parks and attractions, than put up with cuts at Disney, then Disney will have a reason to open its checkbook to win back its former customers. But if fans continue to support Disney's theme parks — deciding that Disney with cuts is still better than the competition — then why of Earth should Disney increase marginal spending on labor and operations? It's making its money without that expense.

Every time Disney raises its ticket prices or cuts something in its parks, fans go online and wail and moan. Many say that's the final straw and that they will stop spending money at Disney's theme parks. And year after year, Disney's theme park attendance and income grow anyway.

Disney knows exactly what it is doing.

Readers respond:

From an anonymous reader: This is spot on. The loss in ESPN subscribers may be impacting other divisions who need to boost their bottom line so overall the consolidated [profit/loss] for the Walt Disney Company is in line with forecasts. However I've always been skeptical of the blame Shanghai movement for the reasons you outlined. Has no impact on the P/L. Perhaps it impacts the cash flow statement, but Disney is probably borrowing the money anyways so balance sheet ratios stay in line.

Why I'm Rooting for Shanghai Disneyland, and You Should Be Too

First published June 15, 2016, by Bryan Schreier

It's no surprise to anyone who frequents Theme Park Insider

that June 16th marks the official grand opening for Shanghai Disneyland, Disney's largest and most expensive theme park ever. But any excitement that exists seems to be marred with skepticism, apathy and even anger.

Why? Well here are just a few of the reasons, speculations, facts(?) that are leaving a bad taste in many Disney fanboys' (and girls') mouths. I can't speculate or even substantiate any of these, but here are just a few:

1. Shanghai Disneyland has absorbed a sizable piece of the entire Parks and Resorts budget for going on a decade now, at the expense of the stateside parks.
2. Shanghai Disneyland is over budget and missed its planned opening date by almost a year, causing expense optimization protocols at other Disney parks to make-up for it.
3. Shanghai Disneyland opens with a slew of brand-new, never before built rides and attractions, using technology that we currently do not at stateside Disney parks.
4. Shanghai is (and has been) Disney CEO Bob Iger's major focus for Parks and Resorts, not Disneyland or Walt Disney World.
5. The construction of Shanghai Disneyland caused delays in the building, expanding and/or re-imagining of stateside parks.

But IMHO this should be an exciting time for any Disney Parks fan, and here's why.

First, remember that a success in Shanghai means everyone wins. Iger, the Disney Company as a whole, you, me, everyone. The fact of the matter is that anything that contributes to the Parks and Resorts division revenue makes Wall Street happy, and when Wall Street is happy, we get to reap the rewards. The larger the Parks and Resorts division becomes, the more visibility, funding and importance is placed on it. So (in theory), if Shanghai is a success, that means more money for the entire division, which means more new rides, lands, and expansions for us. If Shanghai were to fail or miss expectations, more money will be funneled to fix it, which means less for everyone else.

Second, like him or not (I happen to), Shanghai is Bob's baby. His contract was extended (in part) so he could see Shanghai through to grand opening, now that it is here, I speculate one of two things will happen: either Bob will finally vacate his post (soonest would be 2018, due to the latest extension ask from the board) thus bringing in some new blood which should make a lot of Iger-haters happy, or he will continue on indefinitely as CEO. Now, this next statement won't win me any new friends, but I happen to think that Bob is more of a parks guy than most people. Yes, we went through a rough time where everything at every park started to stagnate, especially stateside. We watched in horror as the parks went underfunded and Disney began to fail to live up to its own lofty standards. But remember that we are in an unprecedented time of expansion for Disney parks... yes, even stateside. Pandora, Cars Land, Re-imagining Disney's Hollywood Studios, Disney Springs, Hong Kong Disneyland expansion, Ratatouille, Shanghai, Disney Cruise ship revamps (and two new ships coming) all came out of the Iger era. So let's give Bob a little credit, I think he likes parks more than his actions show. Also remember, that under Bob, Parks and Resorts overall operating revenue has reached its highest levels ever, and now accounts for over 30% of total Disney Company business. So say what you will, but I'm with Bob.

Lastly, all of the effort, skill and innovation that has brought Shanghai Disneyland to life is a great asset to Disney and us theme park fans. It's only a matter of time until we see the learnings from Shanghai brought to stateside parks. Disney has done several things for the first-time ever over in China, and now (or soon), the team over in China will come back, hopefully with some amazing things to implement here in the U.S. Can you imagine if DHS phase 3 included a 'Treasure Cove' or 'Adventure Isle' with a clone of the Indiana Jones Adventure ride, Pirates Battle for Sunken Treasure and an updated Indy Stunt Show? Just sayin'.

So whatever your opinions are, let's agree that from what we've seen, Disney brought its A+ game to China. As for Disney, I'm wishing them well in China and looking forward to them bringing that A+ game back to the states. As for me, I'm going to re-watch YouTube on-ride videos of Pirates and Tron Lightcycles… for the hundredth time and smile ear to ear.

First Impressions from Visiting Shanghai Disneyland
First published June 18, 2016, by Renata Primavera

SHANGHAI — After months of preparation and anticipation, the day has finally come: I was fortunate enough to attend Shanghai Disneyland both on its grand opening date and on the 17th. We've got a lot of ground to cover on this new venture by Disney, so I've decided to divide my report on the park into smaller sections.

The opening day itself

Although regular visitors, such as myself, weren't able to attend the official ceremonies carried out by Bob Iger and company, a lot of surprises were in store as the special day went by.

I started my day at 10am at the park's turnstile, where they sent me to exchange my printed tickets for actual ones. After that, I was sent to a waiting zone — a place near the entrance where I was greeted by very happy cast members handing out a special package containing a grand opening button and postcard, a park map (mine in English), and a band with my waiting zone location written on it. It was there, in waiting zone 1B, that I waited for about two hours for the time when I could enter the park. The band not only showed the order in which my section would be allowed inside the park — it was a first-come, first-in basis — but also provided a way for anyone to go to the toilet or buy a snack and then come back in.

All very organized, as was the entrance itself. At exactly 11:50am, a massive tunnel of cast members directed us to the park, greeting all of us effusively as we finally entered Shanghai

Disneyland for the first time. I had two special encounters during this: one was meeting my ex-manager from my days as a cast member at Magic Kingdom's Frontierland, a huge coincidence; the other, was running into Bob Iger, the man himself, with a smile on his face, leaving the park and waving at everyone who recognized him — to my surprise, a lot of Chinese did!

Other small gifts were given throughout the day. At the biggest attractions, certificates were handed out when you left, saying congratulations for being the first people to ride it — Tron, Pirates of the Caribbean and Peter Pan being among them. Cast members also gave "grand opening" stickers in different colors as guests passed them by at a ride or store.

At the end of the day, after the Ignite the Dream nighttime show took place, a special fireworks show featuring what I assume were traditional Chinese songs, I could see lots of Chinese guests feeling emotional with it — a sight that is most uncommon around these parts for sure.

But more than perks, gifts, and special shows, the highlight of the opening day was the energy one could feel anywhere around the park. Everyone was so excited to be there, and cast members' energy and happiness towards the guests was at an all-time high. If you could ever use the word "magical moment" at a Disney park, this grand opening would be it.

Overview of the park

The park's much-talked-about five billion dollar budget did not go to waste. Unlike Hong Kong Disneyland or Disney California Adventure, which were received with negative reviews on their opening, Shanghai Disneyland feels like a complete park, not something put together in a hurry. It is impressive in many ways, starting with its size. It is spacious, so even when it is crowded, you don't feel like it is.

Also its lands... oh, the lands. The level of detail is definitely going to appeal to anyone, even the ones who don't particularly pay attention to that when visiting a theme park. At Treasure Cove, for example, there are tiny references and photo spots everywhere you look. And this version of Tomorrowland finally might have settled the problem of the area by settling on a décor focused on neon and silver and attractions that don't try to predict the future, only send us to universe unlike ours.

With all that being said, it is important to stress that this is a Chinese theme park, for Chinese guests. Even though all signs are in both Mandarin and English, the vast majority of cast members don't speak English fluently. Some even had this to say when I tried talking to them: "Sorry, I don't speak English." They make up for this with much sympathy and perseverance, and I never left a place without having my question answered. However, I do not recommend this park for travel beginners, definitely.

The language can also be a drawback in some attractions, since they are all spoken in Mandarin. On Pirates of the Caribbean, the visual elements speak for themselves and you kind of get what is going on. But Stitch Encounter, on the other hand, in which the alien interacts directly with the audience, is useless. Everyone is laughing around you and you just nod and smile, without understanding what is going on.

The main attractions

Let's get down to business and talk about the main stars of the park. First let me start by saying that I was impressed with the variety of rides at Shanghai. There were great options of dark rides, mild attractions, something for kids, and something a bit more intense. Overall, a great mix for a Magic Kingdom-style park.

Two of them are tied up as the number one attraction at Shanghai Disneyland. In alphabetical order, I shall begin with the new take of a beloved classic, Pirates of the Caribbean Battle for the Sunken Treasure.

It feels like good old Pirates at the beginning, with the Barbossa's Bounty restaurant taking Blue Bayou's place at our right, followed by a talking skull as we enter a dark cave. There's a perfect nod to the original ride, with the three pirates and a dog scene recreated with a dark twist: they all died while waiting for the damn key! It looks as though it will be more of the same until, right in front of you, magic happens and a simple skeleton becomes Jack Sparrow's talking Audio-Animatronic. (I've ridden it three times, and still wasn't able to find out how that piece of visual effect happens!) From then on, we are sent to the bottom of the sea, where we glimpse the sunken treasures and meet the evil Davy Jones (another amazing Audio-Animatronic), which then send us back up into the middle of the naval battle.

The sheer size of each scene is unlike any other Pirates attraction in the world. Take the battle scene in the other ones and multiply them by 10 and you get close to the scale of this new version. But that alone does not make for an excellent ride. In this case, the use of Audio-Animatronics, actual scenery, and screens is its triumph for sure, putting us right in the middle of the action like never before. Let's forget for one second the whole "Universal vs. Disney using screens" discussion, and see screens for what they really are — another set of tools Imagineers and creators alike now have to help them tell a great story in a ride. And that is what was accomplished brilliantly here.

Last, but not least, I have to give it to the person that decided not to use Pirates' regular track. The boat goes forward, backwards, and turns from side to side, whatever it takes so you don't miss out on one single thing in this spectacular attraction.

On the other side of the park lies TRON Lightcycle Power Run (I will never understand Disney's need for these long names...), a roller coaster that appeals to both thrill-seeking guests and fans of well-themed rides.

Even if you couldn't care less for the movie franchise, this is a guaranteed hit. The idea is that we are being scanned into the game world portrayed in the movies, where we will race in high-speed lightcycles as part of the blue team, opposite three other teams. This is all shown in the line — one of the best in the park — all in blue neon and showing us how the guests are being accelerated in the roller coaster, as we anticipate when it will be our turn. Finally is it our turn and we sit on the bikes that turned out to be not so uncomfortable as expected. We are first sent to a short exterior track, then into the building, where we have to race through eight blue neon circles to win the battle.

Disney claims it is one of the fastest coasters in any of its park, and it does feel that way. Even without any loops and twists, the speed is what guarantees the thrill factor here, combined with the uniqueness of riding a roller coaster on a motorbike and, once again, its great theming.

Coming in a close second? Another exclusive ride of Shanghai, Voyage to the Crystal Grotto. As you sail among beautiful gardens and a great view of the Enchanted Storybook Castle, you are met by "dancing" sculptures and fountains displaying Disney's classics, including Aladdin, Tangled, Fantasia and most deserving Mulan, who is featured extensively throughout the park. It's simples and delightful at the same time, with an ending inside the castle that makes it truly unique. A great example of what a Fantasyland ride can be.

A bit of disappointment, for me, was the Roaring Rapids. The mountain where it is set in is truly beautiful (another point for Disney's mountains!), but I was expecting something with more story. The scenery is pretty, there's a lot of suspense up until you face the monster, and Q'araq is an amazing Audio-Animatronic, even scary! But that, plus a nice drop at the end, are it. I was hoping for more storytelling like the Popeye & Bluto's Bilge-Rat Barges ride in Universal's Islands of Adventure and less Kali River Rapids, and it ends somewhere in the middle. Not enough for me.

Other highlights at Shanghai Disneyland Park are the improved Peter Pan's Flight — also using a great mix of Animatronics and screens — and Buzz Lightyear Planet Rescue. As a fan of Animation Academy, I was thrilled to see a version of it in the Marvel Universe area, where I had the chance to draw a Spider-Man. (it is mostly in Mandarin, but I was able to understand it all through the screen.)

Eating and shopping

I felt overwhelmed at the food choices in the park. About 70% of what you find is Asian-inspired, and, as fan of it, I was thrilled. On the first day I had lunch at the Wandering Moon Teahouse, the most Chinese of the options, located in the Gardens of Imagination. Surrounded by a Chinese setting, I ordered an Eight Treasure Duck — a seasoned Duck with rice, vegetables and other ingredients I could not identify. Delicious. To drink, a Peach Ice Tea which sounds simple, but was very tasty. Too bad the souvenir cup in the shape of a Bamboo was not available.

The next day, I had lunch at the Tangled Tree Tavern, with Asian and Western options. I opted for the Sichuan Chicken with fries, a kind of Chinese take on the Fish and Chips, and it was really, really good. Once again, I decided to drink something "local" and ordered a honey slushy with berries, which was tasteful, but more of a dessert.

Speaking of desserts, my favorite place to eat at Shanghai was definitely Remy's Patisserie, on Mickey Avenue. This bakery had great snacks options such as baked pastries and croissants, and some of the most beautiful looking sweets I've seen recently. It was an ordeal to pick just one, so I ended up having three of them during the two days: a raspberry eclair, a lemon tart and New York cheesecake — all to die for. Also, if you looking for a caffeine fix, they serve a decent espresso here. (I'm Brazilian; espressos are always on the lookout for me!)

If you don't feel like eating Asian... pizzas, burgers, corn dogs, turkey legs, and others can be found. Except for popcorn, which is only sold with caramel flavor (how I missed the regular popcorn these two days).

In terms of merchandise, Americans and Europeans will have a blast here. Although prices are high like any other Disney park, when you convert to Dollars and Euros, they became cheap — very cheap. It's your chance to stock up on traditional Disney products such as T-shirts, pens, stuffed animals, and also some Asian-style souvenirs, such as Tsum-Tsum and Duffy dolls!

All in all, if you are a theme park fan in general, start saving now for a trip to Shanghai Disneyland. You won't regret it, for sure, and you can always pair it with a trip to Hong Kong or Tokyo!

How to Plan Your Visit to Shanghai Disneyland
First published June 15, 2016

You've watched the attraction videos and seen the opening gala. Now, if you're wanting to plan a trip to see the new Shanghai Disneyland in person, here are your next steps.

Step 1: Get a visa

Most Theme Park Insider readers can travel to Disney's theme parks in France and Japan (and sometimes Hong Kong) without needing to get a visa in addition to their passport. But China does not (for the most part) allow visa-free travel into the country for Americans, Canadians, or citizens of the U.K. That means that you will have to apply for and obtain a visa before booking travel to Shanghai Disneyland.

If you are an American and live in the Washington, D.C., New York, Chicago, Houston, San Francisco, or Los Angeles areas, this might be easier than if you don't. China requires you to apply, pay for, and pick up your visa in person at its embassy or consulates, which are located in those cities. Go to www.china-embassy.org/eng/visas/hrsq for instructions. If you don't want to or can't take the time to apply in person, you will need to hire an agency to apply on your behalf. Check with your local auto club, if you are a member, or a local travel agency, if there are any left in your community. Otherwise, hit Google and search for "China visa" and take your pick of agencies. A visa costs $140 for American citizens, in addition to whatever agency fees you end up needing to pay if you don't apply in person.

Sound like a hassle? There is another way.

Alternate Step 1: Don't get a visa

China allows visa-free travel into the country for Americans and residents of many other countries who are transiting through Shanghai on their way to another country. You can stay in Shanghai up to 144 hours before you have to depart, and if you do, you won't need to obtain a visa in advance.

Here's the catch, though: This exemption is for transit visitors. That means you cannot fly into Shanghai and return to the same country. You must fly onto a different country when leaving Shanghai than the one from which you flew into Shanghai. And the transit visa exemption is good only when you fly directly into Shanghai. You can't make your connection in Beijing first.

So you'll have to book your airfare to Shanghai as part of a multi-city "open jaw" trip, rather than a traditional round-trip ticket. I use the "multiple destinations" option on Momondo.com to check airfares for trips such as this. For Disney fans, I'd suggest visiting Japan as the third country for a visa-free Shanghai Disneyland trip, then flying from Shanghai to Tokyo to visit Tokyo Disneyland and DisneySea. (Talk about a dream vacation!)

Whatever itinerary you select, make sure that it does not force you into connecting through Beijing. If you travel there, even for a connection, you will need to have applied for a Chinese visa.

Also remember that the clock starts ticking on your 144 hours as soon as your flight arrives. Your scheduled departure from Shanghai must be within 144 hours of your flight's arrival time for you to qualify for the visa exemption.

Step 2: Find a place to stay

Your easiest option is to stay at one of the two official, on-site hotels at the Shanghai Disneyland Resort: the Disneyland Hotel or the Toy Story Hotel. Both are run by Disney and rates start at about US$130 a night for the Toy Story Hotel and about $286 a night for the Disneyland Hotel. If you don't want to stay on-site, you can find several hotels from western chains with lower nightly rates in the area, though the expense and travel time to and from the park might not make them a better deal than staying on site. You can book Shanghai Disneyland's hotels through its website, www.shanghaidisneyresort.com/en.

Step 3: Get your tickets

Again, you'll want to go to the official Shanghai Disneyland website to buy your tickets in advance. As with other Disney theme parks now, admission ticket prices vary by the date of visit, and tickets might not be available at the front gate on your date of visit if you do not buy them in advance. High-season tickets cost $77 a day, so fans of Disney's U.S. theme parks should see this as a bargain anyway.

You also might want to download the official Shanghai Disneyland app to buy and store your tickets, check wait times, and navigate your way around the park. The app looks and works much like the official Disneyland app for the Anaheim park. Shanghai Disneyland also offers Fastpass ride reservations, but no Disney World-style advance reservation Fastpass+.

Step 4: Make your other arrangements

Do you have special dietary needs? Traveling with disabilities? Wondering what to pack? Shanghai Disneyland has you covered. Go to www.shanghaidisneyresort.com/en/guest-services for the help you need. Temperatures in Shanghai range from 50 degrees (Fahrenheit) in winter to the 90s in summer. Humidity is definitely a thing, as is China's notorious air pollution. Dress appropriately, and plan to get inside and rest when you need it.

Step 5: Get to the park

Shanghai Disneyland has its own stop on the Shanghai Metro rail system, but if you're flying in to Pudong International Airport, frankly, it looks as if you could walk to Shanghai Disney in not much more time than it would take to navigate the rail network. So your best bet appears to be to hail a taxi at the airport and let it drive you to the resort, which is about 15 miles away from Pudong airport. If you're staying off-site, check to see if your hotel has a shuttle from the airport, or one to the park for that matter.

And finally, remember to submit your photos and attraction and restaurant ratings to www.themeparkinsider.com/reviews/shanghai_disneyland when you return, to help other Insiders plan their Shanghai Disneyland vacations.

ORLANDO AND THE TERRIBLE, HORRIBLE, NO-GOOD, VERY BAD SUMMER

After several years of strong attendance gains, Orlando theme parks began 2016 with optimism. Universal Orlando would open a new ride based on its classic King Kong character and Walt Disney World would debut a new slate of night-time experiences at Disney's Animal Kingdom. SeaWorld was looking to reverse its attendance woes with the closest thing to a sure bet in the attractions industry — a brand-new Bolliger & Mabillard Hyper Coaster. What possibly could go wrong?

Since you are a theme park fan, you know that the moment in a ride when you get this feeling is often the moment when it all *really does* start to go terribly wrong. And it did in 2016 in Orlando. But adversity creates the opportunity to show hidden strength. As Universal Creative Vice President Thierry Coup told us once about adversity, "It gives us a chance to be heroes, and to try to save the day."

And, ultimately, the people of the Orlando theme park community did pull together in 2016.

How Will Orlando Theme Parks React to the Pulse Nightclub Shooting?

First published June 12, 2016

If you haven't yet heard the horrible news, a gunman killed 49 people in an Orlando nightclub early this morning — focusing the world's attention on Central Florida in a most unwelcome way. The shooting — now the deadliest recent mass shooting inside the United States — came one day after another shooting in Orlando that attracted international headlines, the killing of singer Christina Grimmie.

In both cases, according to local police, the shooters were not from Orlando, but came to the city to carry out their attacks. Obviously, that's troubling for everyone in the Orlando area. No one wants the community to become an attractive target for outside criminals and terrorists. Nor does anyone in the tourism industry want the public to begin conflating easily the words "Orlando" and "shooting," and thereby reconsider their vacation plans to the area.

The Pulse nightclub, frequented by members of the local LGBT community, was located on South Orange Avenue, well way from the traditional tourist zones of the city. But it certainly was known and frequented by cast and team members of the Walt Disney World and Universal Orlando resorts, as well as employees of other area attractions. We've not seen a list of the victims, but it is hard to imagine that cast and team members will not be among them.

The challenge today is to embrace and comfort the survivors, and the friends of families of the lost. Then, to promote and ensure the continued safety of all other residents and visitors to the area. It's a rough, rough day today in Orlando. But here's our message to our friends throughout the community — we're all here for you, no matter where we are.

Readers react:

From Shaun Fisher: Several years ago on the news in Portland, Oregon, a man woke up to put some coffee on. He then returned to his room, only to find a stream of light that had gone through his roof, ceiling, pillow, mattress, and into the floor. A small meteorite had made the hole. He was grateful to have made his coffee that morning. I tell you this story so you can see that even staying home can be dangerous. This is an ugly world, but it's also a beautiful world. Don't let things like this change your plans. Go and live your lives. Visit theme parks. Treat your kids. This is horrible and sad, but we can't put our lives on hold because of it. Some of my best memories center around theme parks, and now that I'm a father, I'm continuing that tradition that my parents made before me. For me, Disney and Universal is all about love (a lot of money, too). I'll keep traveling and keep living my life.

AJ Hummel: This is a very tragic event, and my thoughts go out to those present at the club, as well as the families of the victims. It is unacceptable that this type of incident happens as frequently as it does, but unfortunately there is very little that can be done to prevent it. The elimination of terrorism would require global change, and sadly that is highly unlikely to happen. As for modifying travel plans, I'll just say this: I do not currently have any plans to visit Orlando, but if I did I would not change them. One isolated incident is not an indication of increased danger because an isolated incident can occur anywhere. The goal of terrorism is to place terror into a population, and the best way to fight that is to avoid being terrified and go on with life. In my opinion, if a terrorist commits a horrible act and one percent of the population changes their daily routine due to it, the terrorist has won. Besides, there are things the average person does on a daily basis that, according to statistics, they should be much more afraid of.

Sarah Warner: A terribly sad event! My heart goes out to all the families and those who witnessed the events unfolding first hand. For the city of Orlando and especially the LGBT community, my heart feels such pain. Orlando is a wonderful destination for everyone but sometimes not even Disney magic can hide the reality of hatred that surrounds us.

Theme Parks, Fans Rally in Support of Orlando Victims and Survivors
First published June 14, 2016

After maintaining silence since Sunday morning's rampage at a nightclub in Orlando, Disney Parks' social media accounts have returned to announce Disney's $1 million donation to a new fund set up to assist the victims of the attack.

Orlando mayor Buddy Dyer announced the creation of the OneOrlando fund to "raise and receive money to help those families most affected by the tragic events." Anyone can donate to the fund via www.oneorlando.org, and Disney has announced that it will match donations made by its cast members.

Disney CEO Bob Iger had issued a brief statement of condolence after the attack, but it was sent to a handful of old media outlets and not published on the Disney Parks' blog, Twitter, or Facebook accounts, which made no posts between the time of the attacks and this morning's announcement. Universal Orlando, however, did post a note, following the announcement that one of its team members had been among the victims.

Universal Orlando team members and fans honored Luis Vielma, who had worked on the Harry Potter and the Forbidden Journey ride, with a wand raising moment in front of Hogwarts Castle last night.

Many other cast and team members at the Orlando parks have been posting to social media to show their support for the Orlando community, and especially to the gay and lesbian community members targeted in the attack. And SeaWorld Orlando this morning posted photos of its employees' shows of support to its official social media accounts.

Universal Orlando teams members Luis Vielma and Xavier Serrano and Walt Disney World cast member Jerald Arthur Wright were among the 49 people killed in the shooting at the Pulse nightclub in Orlando early Sunday morning — the largest mass shooting in recent American history.

Gator Drags Child into Water at Disney's Seven Seas Lagoon
First published June 15, 2016

As a parent, this is nightmare fuel. And after everything that's happened in Orlando this week...

Here's the story: An alligator reportedly attacked and carried a toddler into the water of the Seven Seas Lagoon, near Disney's Grand Floridian Resort this evening. The Grand Floridian was showing a movie on the beach tonight, and it appears that the toddler and its family were watching the movie when the attack happened. Various eyewitnesses quoted on Twitter reported seeing a 7-foot gator.

At a 1am (ET) press conference, the Orange County (FL) Sheriff said that 50 law enforcement personnel were on the scene, looking for the two-year-old boy from Nebraska, who had not yet been recovered. He said that multiple witnesses saw the incident and that the parents entered the water trying to rescue their child, who had been playing at the edge of the water.

Update (Wed. morning): Still no sign of the child, although authorities have found four gators so far. Ferry service to and from the Magic Kingdom has been suspended for the duration of the search.

Update (Wed. afternoon): Authorities have recovered the body of the boy, now identified as Lane Graves, the son of Matt and Melissa Graves of Elkhorn, Neb. We send all of our condolences to the family.

Walt Disney World President George A. Kalogridis issued this statement: "There are no words to convey the profound sorrow we feel for the family and their unimaginable loss. We are devastated and heartbroken by this tragic accident and are doing what we can to help them during this difficult time.

"On behalf of everyone at Disney, we offer them our deepest sympathy."

The first reports of the attack sparked a social media firestorm of blame, as often happens as people try to cope with the shock of such a terrible event. Eventually, that evolved into a debate over what Disney ought to do to accommodate both its guests and the local wildlife. Ultimately, as I predicted below, Disney did end up building walls and fences around many of its creeks and lakes in public areas to separate visitors from alligators and other potentially dangerous wildlife.

Readers react:

TH Creative: In Florida, asking Disney to stop alligators from getting into the lakes is like asking Disney to stop squirrels from getting into trees.

Robert Niles: I imagine that this also will force Disney to create a defined perimeter around waterways currently open to guest access around the resort. And to post more explicit warning signs. After all, many people from outside Central Florida don't understand that if you're looking at a body of water in Orlando, you can just assume there's a gator in it.

Chad H: I lived in Far North Queensland for a while, where crocodiles pose the same threat, but mostly just to those in unfamiliar waterways, so I can see this from the local and outsider perspective. When you live with a danger in your "back yard" you learn how to manage the risk... Most I'm sure wouldn't think twice about a bucket collecting rainwater for example, live in the tropics and you see it as a breeding ground for mosquitos carrying awful diseases. A Floridian might naturally shy away from unfamiliar waterways, but a visitor from Chicago for example doesn't see waterway as a threat (in the same way at least). However, this is an area where Disney is a victim of its own success. It has a reputation for family fun in a safe environment - be it a movie, a theme park, Disney vacation, cruise, etc, parents expect a sort of walled child safe garden, so to speak, so perhaps aren't even looking for threats at all.

TH Creative: The loss of a child for whatever reason is a heartbreaking situation. Having said this, and while at the same time expressing full understanding and sympathy for the family's immeasurable grief: If the child had died in a car accident on WDW property (equally tragic) would the story have been the lead on every network news program? For that matter, had the alligator attack been somewhere in Florida other than WDW property, would it be getting this level of attention?

How to Stay Safe in a Theme Park: Respect the Local Wildlife
First published June 15, 2016

We've long worked to educate visitors about staying safe in theme parks. While the most dangerous part of a theme park visit remains getting to and from the park itself, your time inside a theme park resort is not entirely risk free. But with a little common sense and some knowledge, the odds are overwhelming that you'll suffer no physical harm while visiting a park or its surrounding resort.

But as we saw last night at Walt Disney World, accidents happen. For those who haven't yet heard the news, an alligator attacked a two-year-old boy who was playing at the edge of the water of the Seven Seas Lagoon, next to Disney's Grand Floridian Resort. The boy's father went into the water to try to wrestle the child from the gator, but failed.

The family who lost their child last night was from Nebraska. I've lived in Omaha and in Orlando and never once did I think that anything potentially fatal was lurking under the surface of any pond, lake, or stream in Nebraska. But Florida is different. Most people who live in Central Florida understand you just ought to assume that any body of water large enough to hold a gator actually has a gator in it. Yet visitors from up north don't know that. Disney posts signs around the Seven Seas Lagoon prohibiting swimming in the lake, but the warning signs don't mention gators or wildlife. Visitors who assume the warning is just Disney's attempt to escape liability for drownings due so at grave risk they don't know they're taking.

So to our list of theme park safety tips, let's add this: Respect the local wildlife.

Step one toward doing that is acknowledging that you don't know about the local wildlife. Don't assume that the woods, water, fields, beach, or desert in the place you are visiting are the same as yours at home. Vacation destinations can help by posting warning signs or distributing information at check-in about the local wildlife and the risks associated with them. I just returned from a visit to Yellowstone National Park, and believe me, the park officials there were aggressive in warning people about the wildlife in the park. Travelers need hosts in all other vacation destinations with local wildlife to be just as aggressive about informing their guests, too.

This isn't just for the protection of visitors. A week before my visit to Yellowstone, a clueless family loaded a baby bison into the back of their car because they feared it was getting too cold. Rangers eventually had to put down the bison calf after its herd rejected it.

Respecting wildlife means understanding that these animals are wild. They are not pets and should not be treated as domesticated animals. So keep your distance. Do not approach or try to interact with the animals. If a wild animal approaches you, you need to know the correct response to avoid provoking the animal to attack, then as best you can, try to move away to give the animal the space it deserves. Remember that federal law protects many species of wild animals and prohibits contact with them.

Respecting wildlife also means that you should never attempt to feed them. It sickened me to read in the Orlando Sentinel's report that some Disney guests have been feeding the wild alligators on property. This is beyond stupid. Feeding animals conditions them to seek contact with human beings, with potentially disastrous results. Feeding wild alligators is against the law in Florida. We'd love to see Disney start backing this up by ejecting and permanently banning from its property any guests found to be feeding alligators on Walt Disney World property, as well.

Last night's tragedy exposed that too few visitors to Central Florida know the risks associated with local wildlife. It's not the fault of this family, who have suffered an unimaginable loss. No one told them.

So we're telling you now. Spread the word. For your safety — as well as the safety of wild animals — respect the local wildlife in all of your travels.

Parents Won't Sue Disney over Alligator Attack
First published July 20, 2016

The parents of a Nebraska toddler who was killed in a gator attack near the Grand Floridian Resort earlier this summer will not file a lawsuit against Disney.

The family of Lane Graves issued the following statement to the press:

"Melissa and I are broken. We will forever struggle to comprehend why this happened to our sweet baby, Lane. As each day passes, the pain gets worse, but we truly appreciate the outpouring of sympathy and warm sentiments we have received from around the world.

"We know that we can never have Lane back, and therefore, we intend to keep his spirit alive through the Lane Thomas Foundation. It is our hope that through the foundation we will be able to share with others the unimaginable love Lane etched in our hearts. In addition to the foundation, we will solely be focused on the future health of our family and will not be pursuing a lawsuit against Disney. For now, we continue to ask for privacy as we focus on our family."

The Orlando Sentinel asked a Walt Disney World spokesperson to confirm that the company had made a settlement with or contribution to the family's new foundation, but WDW president George Kalogridis said in an emailed reply to the paper only that "in the wake of this tragic accident we continue to provide ongoing support for the family."

Disney's knowledge of and policies toward wild alligators became an important part of the story in the days following the fatal attack. That attention drew a great deal of traffic to a blog post from 2009, in which I described my experience as a cast member encountering wild alligators on the dock at Tom Sawyer Island in the Magic Kingdom. This story also is featured in our book "Stories from a Theme Park Insider."

Theme Park Cast Member Stories: Sometimes, Mother Nature Runs the Show
First published June 15, 2009

The people who design and build theme parks create powerful, immersive environments. The scale of engineering involved can be immense. The apparent "ground level" of Walt Disney World's Magic Kingdom, for example, is actually the second story of a massive complex, built upon a series of "tunnels" that were built at the actual level of the ground. Earth was excavated from what became the Seven Seas Lagoon, piled around the tunnels, and the Magic Kingdom built on top of that.

We often joked at the Magic Kingdom that the tallest mountain in Florida was Disney's Big Thunder Mountain, a fake peak built by Disney's contractors. (This was before Splash Mountain, so that might be the joke now.) Regardless, starting from when you board the ferry at the Transportation and Ticket Center and sail across the Seven Seas Lagoon, all the way through your day in the Magic Kingdom, whether you take a boat around the Rivers of America or ascend Big Thunder, every body of water you see and every landscape you cross will be 100-percent, completely, totally man-made.

But from time to time, Mother Nature reminds cast members they cannot completely dismiss her will. The afternoon thunderstorms provide one example. We often found others working the rafts at Tom Sawyer's Island.

TSI rarely failed to open at its designated time each morning, when I worked there. The rafts typically opened an hour after the park, partly because it wasn't exactly the most popular attraction in the Magic Kingdom, but mostly because no work could be done on the island, to stock the restaurant or do any required maintenance work, until the sun came up. Unlike every other location in the park, the island had no artificial street light, which is why the island closes at dusk. With no artificial lights for the third shift, work had to wait until sun-up, so we waited until 10 am to open the island to guests.

The lead still showed up at 7:30, though, as he or she would be needed to ferry some of the maintenance and food workers across the river. Custodial had a Jon boat that they used to take trash off the island, but everyone else relied on the rafts. I arrived for my lead shift several minutes early one morning, carrying the box of doughnuts and the morning paper that I used as bait to ensure both that my morning crew would be on time and that supervisors would drop in, when I could confront them with the list of show quality repairs that I wanted approved.

But this morning, as I turned the corner onto the TSI mainland dock, I immediately knew that this wouldn't be a normal morning at TSI. Not with a very large alligator - and her kids - sunning themselves on the dock.

I froze and hid the doughnuts behind my back (I have no idea whether gators like doughnuts, and had no inclination to find out). Slowly, I backed up, and walked the long way around the TSI cabin, so I could get into the office from the queue exit.

I called Animal Control.

"Um, we've got three alligators on the Tom Sawyer's Island raft dock. Could you send someone down?"

"On the island or the mainland?"

"Mainland."

"Oooookay."

While I waited for animal control to show up, I called the opening supervisor. No need for doughnuts today, I figured I'd soon have every suit in the Magic Kingdom on my dock regardless.

Well, not actually on the dock, but near it. Okay, a respectable distance away. But they'd be looking at the dock.

Within five minutes, I was hosting a little morning get-together for two animal control guys, two attractions supervisors, the area manager, and a merchandise supervisor who walked over to see what the fuss was about.

One of the attractions supervisors turned to one of the animal control guys.

"So, how soon can you move those alligators so that we can open?"

The animal control guys exploded with laughter.

"Sorry, we don't move gators. They get to stay as loooong as they want."

The attractions supervisors looked a bit queasy.

"You want to know when you'll be open?" the other animal control guy asked, as he nodded toward the attractions supervisors. "Go on down and ask the gator!"

So when the park opened that morning, Tom Sawyer's Island became Disney's Gatorland, and the raft drivers became crowd control, managing the flow of guests who lined up along the riverside walkway to gawk at Mrs. Gator and her young-'uns. Around 10:15, the gators had had enough, slipped into the water and swam away.

We waited another 20 minutes before we opened the ride. Just in case the gators decided to come back.

Because, you know, sometimes Mother Nature runs the show.

Orlando-area Parks and Visitors Prepare for Hurricane Matthew
First published October 4, 2016

If you're visiting the Orlando area theme parks this week, get ready to welcome another special guest during your stay — Hurricane Matthew.

Wednesday morning update: The Orlando area is now under a hurricane warning, with the eye of the storm expected to brush the shore near Cape Canaveral sometime Friday morning. Matthew weakened as it passed over eastern Cuba and is now a Category 3 storm, but it is expected to strengthen as it passes through the Bahamas today and tomorrow.

Visitors should expect high winds — possibly hurricane force — and heavy rain as the storm moves through the theme park area on Friday. We expect airlines soon to begin canceling flights in the southeast on Thursday through the weekend, so if your travel plans include a flight in Florida, Georgia, or the Carolinas over the next four days, check with your airline and be prepared for flight cancellations.

All schools in Central Florida have canceled classes for Thursday and Friday, and colleges are canceling and rescheduling games this weekend — including the University of Central Florida, which has postponed its scheduled Friday night game in Orlando. We've not yet heard about park closures at Walt Disney World or Universal Orlando, but Disney is offering to move guests out of the Fort Wilderness campground, Polynesian bungalows and Saratoga Springs Treehouse villas, which are the most exposed lodging properties at the resort. Reports also have SeaWorld Orlando closing at 2pm Thursday and all day Friday. Legoland Florida will be closed on Friday.

If you're stuck in the area, you'll probably want to join the crowds at local supermarkets if you need to stock up on food and water to get you through the weekend. The theme park hotels will do their best to maintain critical operations during the storm — including at least limited food service — but remember that the staff will be a ride-out crew if the storm's too intense for regularly scheduled staff to get to work.

If your personal or rental car is going to be parked outside during the storm, go take photos of it now, as those photos will help in any insurance claim if the storm damages the car.

Theme park fans around the world send their best wishes to everyone in Central Florida right now. We hope that Matthew will keep to the east and that everyone will get to enjoy a safe day in the parks, as unusual and weird as it might turn out to be. We also hope that you'll stay in touch with us throughout this week, as best you can.

Disney World, Universal, and Other Orlando Parks Close for Hurricane Matthew
First published October 5, 2016

Here is the current list of closure at the Central Florida theme parks due to the impending arrival of Hurricane Matthew.

Thursday - Blizzard Beach, Fort Wilderness campground closed. SeaWorld closes at 2pm. Walt Disney World and Universal Orlando close at 5pm. Halloween Horror Nights, Mickey's Not So Scary Halloween Party and Spirit of Aloha dinner show canceled.

Friday - Walt Disney World, Universal Orlando, SeaWorld, Legoland, Blizzard Beach, Typhoon Lagoon and Fort Wilderness closed. Halloween Horror Nights, Mickey's Not So Scary Halloween Party and Spirit of Aloha dinner show canceled.

The Orlando area remains under a hurricane warning, its first in more than 10 years, as Hurricane Matthew is expected to brush Florida's east coast late Thursday through Friday, with landfall a possibility in northern Brevard County. The storm has strengthened to Category 4 and is expected to remain at that strength when it reaches the Florida coast.

This is the first time that the Walt Disney World Resort has closed for a hurricane in more than a decade. The Disney World theme parks closed for hurricanes in 1999 and 2004. If you are in Central Florida, make sure you have a safe, well-sheltered place to ride out this major storm. If you have travel plans for the next several days, expect airline cancelations, closures and possible storm damage to disrupt those plans. And if that storm really does come back for seconds, expect even more disruption.

We are sending our best wishes to everyone in the area.

Orlando Area and Theme Parks under Curfew as Hurricane Matthew Strikes
First published October 6, 2016

The Orlando area is under a mandatory curfew now, until 7am on Saturday. It's going to be a long night tonight, and day on Friday, as Hurricane Matthew moves through the area.

All of the local theme parks are closed on Friday, but thousands of people remain on property tonight and tomorrow, staying in and working at the hotels at the Walt Disney World and Universal Orlando resorts. The guests include visitors who could not (or would not) change their travel plans, as well as some Floridians who chose to evacuate to the resorts rather than stay in their homes.

The Orlando area long has been a refuge of choice for Florida residents when hurricanes strike, as people look to flee the coastal areas that bear the most damage in such storms. But this time, it's the Orlando area's turn to face Mother Nature. With the resort areas lying some 40 miles inland, they won't experience the Category 4-force winds that Matthew was packing offshore on Thursday night, but hurricane-force winds and many, many inches of rain are expected.

Hurricane Matthew is forecast to move through the area on Friday, with the weather clearing on Saturday. But this might not be the last that Floridians see of the storm. Due to conditions in the

Atlantic, Matthew is forecast to make a U-turn after moving north off the Georgia shore, with many models showing Matthew returning toward Florida. The storm is forecast to have weakened to a tropical storm by then, but it is possible that the storm could strength back to a hurricane when it reaches warmed waters. So even as the skies clear on Friday night, Orlando-area residents and theme park fans might not yet be in the clear.

This is the first time since 2004 that the parks have closed due to weather, and emotions might be raw as people are confined to homes and hotel rooms — potentially without access to services — for more than a day. Access to food became an issue on Friday evening, as the hotels faced the highly unusual situation of having everyone booked at their properties actually being there at the same time. When a hurricane is raging outside, there's no heading over to another hotel or to the parks for a meal. You're stuck with the food service at your property... along with everyone else.

We are wishing for everyone's continued safety and hope that all our friends can maintain a positive attitude in such a trying situation. And here's a huge "thank you" to all the cast and team members and emergency personnel who are staying on the job during the curfew to provide the assistance than everyone needs.

A few Walt Disney World Resort guests tweeted photos of the $12.99 boxed meal that Disney was selling to guests — a styrofoam clamshell box with a plain, undressed sandwich of lunch meat on white bread, an apple, a small bag of pretzels and a wrapped small cookie. Some visitors complained that Disney had provided better boxed meals for free to stranded guests in 2004.

Meanwhile, other guests reported being able to access at least limited service hotel restaurants. At Universal Orlando, hotels set up buffets in lieu of regular meal service.

Readers respond:

Randy Keith: Disney's meal look like something you would find in a school cafeteria, but for four times the cost. I get that Disney is likely having to pay their employees overtime, but that's no excuse.

Disney should be selling those meals at cost, or $1 more at the most. I hate to criticize a company that I love, but they've gotten ridiculous. Their them park prices are one thing, but overcharging guests when don't have any other food options is a new low. This article shows why staying at a non Disney hotel is the way to go. Universal's meal is overpriced too but at least it isn't a school lunch.

Inuk: FYI, dedicated employees are also riding out the storm at Animal Kingdom, SeaWorld, Discovery Cove, and Aquatica to ensure the safety of the animals that they all care for. Animal Care professions, water quality specialists and divers, maintenance crews, horticulturists, paramedics, and security personnel and stay at the parks to assist in any way possible. Big thanks to all of those passionate employees as well!

Chad H: Was that a Disney meal, or the worlds worst airline food? I can't tell the difference.

From an anonymous reader: Now you wished you were stranded at the local Sweet Tomatoes with their $8.99 buffet

AJ Hummel: While those meals are not technically price gouging, it is poor customer service on Disney's part to sell that for the same price as a regular theme park meal. While they are under no obligation to provide food for free (and I wouldn't expect them to), if they sold the same box meal for $5-7 they would probably have received almost no backlash while still likely making a (small) profit.

Curfew Lifted as Orlando Parks Prepare to Reopen after Hurricane Matthew
First published October 7, 2016

Orange County has lifted its curfew as the worst of Hurricane Matthew has moved out of the Orlando area. The storm made a last-minute shift to the east before brushing the Florida coast, allowing much of Central Florida to escape the extreme winds that had been forecast from the storm. As a result, the areas around

Walt Disney World, Universal Orlando and the rest of the resort areas avoided any major damage.

That's not to say that Matthew didn't have an effect upon the larger area. The winds did blow down trees and knock down power lines, and the rain flooded some areas nearer the Atlantic coast. With flights canceled all day at the Orlando airport, it will take several days for air travel to return to normal, as people scramble to reschedule their flights.

But the area theme parks should be back to normal operation on Saturday, following clean-up of storm debris by ride-out crews today. Universal Orlando and Legoland have announced that they will open tomorrow morning at their regularly scheduled times, all the Walt Disney World parks will open at 8am, and SeaWorld will open at noon. Busch Gardens Tampa remained open during the storm, as Matthew wasn't much more than a typical Florida rainstorm on the state's west coast.

The National Hurricane Center is forecasting that Matthew will continue up the Atlantic coast past Georgia and the Carolinas, before making a wide turn in the Atlantic and returning south to the Bahamas, where it will weaken into a tropical storm and then a tropical depression. If this forecast holds, if Matthew does return to Central Florida, it won't be as anything much more than a typical rainstorm.

Let's hope.

Everything You Need to Know about Disney World and Hurricanes
First published August 12, 2016

A Theme Park Insider reader just wrote to ask about visiting the Walt Disney World Resort during hurricane season. The Atlantic hurricane season officially runs from June 1 through November 30, but late August through September typically seems to be the peak time when hurricanes strike Florida and the rest of the US east and

Gulf coasts.

With many US schools heading back into session in mid- to late August, the next several weeks after that tend to be one of the better times of the year to visit Disney, if you're looking to avoid those big summer crowds. But what about those hurricanes? Let's take a look at some of the things visitors ought to know about Disney World and hurricanes.

1. Yes, Disney World can close during a hurricane

But it almost never happens. The Walt Disney World theme parks have closed for hurricanes in 1999 and 2004. The longest the parks were closed on any one of those occasions was for two days. That's less than a week of lost operation in the nearly 45 years that the resort has been open.

Florida's a big place. While you might read about hurricanes hitting Florida every year, if you pay close attention you'll probably notice that each one always makes landfall someplace different in the state. While the effects of a hurricane may be felt throughout Florida (and the entire southeast!), a direct hit on any one specific location that causes it close is relatively rare.

Especially for a place that is located inland. Remember that the Walt Disney World Resort is located in the Orlando area, nearly an hour inland from the coast. When a hurricane hits land, it begins to lose strength quickly. In practice, when a hurricane is forecast to hit Florida, many Floridians living on or near the coast where the hurricane is forecast to make landfall will evacuate to... Orlando. The huge number of hotel rooms available in the Orlando area during what is typically a slower than normal time for tourism make it an attractive place to retreat and ride out the storm.

2. Even if Disney closes, people still will be there

If the theme parks close, Disney won't kick people out of its hotels. You'll be able to remain there to ride out the storm. And thousands of Disney cast members will remain on the job, staffing the hotels and "battening down the hatches" in the parks and throughout the property. Cast members will remove or secure anything that could blow away or become damaged in the high winds of a hurricane, then remain in place to begin preparing the resort to resume normal operations as soon as possible after the storm passes. Don't expect a full range of services, of course, but you won't be left to fend for yourself in an abandoned resort.

3. If a storm comes, you'll get plenty of warning

Hurricanes aren't earthquakes. Thanks to weather satellites and modern weather forecasting, they no longer strike without warning. You will know days in advance if a hurricane is on track to hit Central Florida, giving you time to adjust your travel plans, if necessary. So watch those forecasts!

4. You can get a refund, if necessary

Walt Disney World's policy is to allow people to cancel without penalty a Walt Disney Travel Company vacation package or room stay booked with Disney if a hurricane warning is issued for the Orlando area — or for your hometown — within seven days of your scheduled arrival. You won't be charged a cancellation or change fee if you cancel, and you will get a full refund of what you've paid. If you wish, you can reschedule to another date without a change fee, although your new reservation will be subject to availability.

If you've booked anything outside Disney, such as airfare, rental cars or rooms elsewhere, you're on your own for those. Check with those providers for their hurricane policies, or consider a travel insurance policy that covers hurricanes. The Universal Orlando Resort has pretty much the same policy for its vacations as Disney — no cancellation or change fees if there's a hurricane warning issued for within seven days of your arrival.

If you decide to take your chances, do prepare for rainy weather. A hurricane might officially miss the Orlando area, but that just means that part of the storm where wind speed reached 75 mph or more failed to hit the community. Wind and rain from the outer bands of the storm might still hit the area. As anyone who's been to Disney during a summer thunderstorm can tell you, some attractions close in stormy weather. Bring a poncho and be ready to be flexible with your plans each day.

5. Florida's used to this

Like we said, Disney will assign cast members to prepare the resort for an incoming storm and to get it ready for normal operation as soon as possible after the storm passes. Businesses and communities in Florida have hurricane plans, and the experience to get through the storm. While places on the coast that sustained the direct hit might be out of commission for a while, that tends not to be an issue in the Orlando area. While you might choose to cancel if your vacation was scheduled for the same week that a hurricane hit, you probably don't have to worry about a vacation scheduled for even a week later. Yes, airlines will need time to work through schedule disruptions, just as they do for a wide variety of summer rain and winter storms. But Disney recovered quickly after the few times in closed in the past and has plans in place to be up and running quickly after the next hurricane strikes, too.

TIMING IS EVERYTHING: THEME PARKS MOVE TO DATE-SPECIFIC PRICING

Theme parks typically raise their prices every year — sometimes twice a year — at Disney and other year-round theme parks. But between those price increases, the cost of buying a ticket to a park has remained the same. It doesn't matter whether you visit on a weekend in July or a weekday in October, the price to get it would be the same.

That changed this year at major theme parks in the United States. Parks began rolling out date-specific prices for one-day tickets, charging more on days expected to draw large crowds, and less on days when crowds were expected to be thin. At this point, market leader Disney offers only three different price tiers and is publishing its rate calendar months in advance, so we're a long way from the real-time dynamic pricing models long used by the airline and hotel industries. Nor does date-specific pricing affect multi-day tickets, which remain the same price no matter when you plan to visit.

But date-specific pricing for one-day tickets gives theme park fans yet another thing to keep in mind as they decide where and when to visit.

Universal Studios Hollywood Starts Rolling Out Date-Specific Pricing on One-Day Tickets
First published December 25, 2015

Universal Studios Hollywood is rolling out the nation's first dynamic pricing structure for one-day tickets to a major theme park, according to multiple reports from readers.

The new pricing structure discounts the price of a one-day ticket purchased online from $5 to $15 off the front-gate price of $95. The amount of the discount — $5, $10, or $15 — depends on the day of the visit, with the biggest discounts typically falling on Tuesdays and Wednesdays. It appears that the price of buying a one-day ticket at the park will remain $95, regardless of the day you visit.

Not all Internet users are seeing the dynamic pricing option, however. Inside Universal reported the change earlier today, but we could not confirm it when we visited Universal Studios Hollywood's website.

We asked our followers on Twitter, and some reported that clicking on Universal's "Buy Tickets Now" link directed them to a page on https://store.universalstudioshollywood.com/, where the dynamic pricing discounts are available, while others were sent to the old pages on https://tickets.universalstudioshollywood.com, where the dynamic pricing is not offered. So it appears random who is getting this option and who is not — at least at this point.

Universal Studios Hollywood Makes Date-Specific Ticket Prices Official
First published February 2, 2016

As we reported earlier, Universal Studios Hollywood is implementing a new daily ticket system where prices will vary depending upon the selected date of your visit.

Under the new system, the front-gate price for a one-day ticket to Universal Studios Hollywood will remain constant. But the discounts the park makes available for buying your ticket online will vary by the date you select for your visit. Of course, this means that you will have to lock in the date of your visit when you buy your ticket online, instead of simply buying and printing a ticket for use on any future date.

Universal made the change official today, after apparently testing the system for some website visitors last month. In today's announcement, Universal also revealed that visitors who buy their tickets online under the new "EZ Rez" system will get early entry to the park starting April 7, the day that The Wizarding World of Harry Potter opens officially.

Given the convenience of buying online, the ability to skip an unnecessary wait at the front gate ticket booths, a discount for buying online, and the ability to get into the Wizarding World before everyone else with early entry crowds it, using EZ Rez to buy your ticket online to Universal Studios Hollywood is as close to a requirement as anything can be for a theme park visitor.

Savings for advance online purchases range from $5 to $20 off the $95 front-gate price, according to our examination of dates now available on the USH website. Universal provides a monthly calendar of available dates and prices when you click to buy tickets on its site, which should also give you a strong indication what crowd levels will be like at the park on any given day. (Cheaper ticket = smaller expected crowd.) Tickets currently are available through the end of September.

With Universal tying advance ticket sales to specific dates, it is now possible for the park to "sell out" certain dates well in advance. How that plays out remains to be seen and depends upon the level at which Universal would cut off sales for a specific date.

Update: If you do not wish to commit to a specific date for your visit, you can buy an undiscounted ticket (same as the gate price) that is not tied to a particular date. Therefore, Universal's new online ticket system ought to be considered more of a dynamic discounting scheme than a dynamic pricing one.

TIMING IS EVERYTHING: THEME PARKS MOVE TO DATE-SPECIFIC PRICING

Readers respond:

Russell Meyer: This is pretty concerning. By effectively forcing guests to schedule theme park visits on specific days, a dangerous precedent is being set. I understand the desire to be able to manage crowds, especially with Potter-mania about to take over USH, but I think going to this extreme is dangerous. People generally plan theme park trips in advance, but the beauty of the experience is the ability to change on the fly. If the weather turns bad, many guests will be upset that they arbitrarily chose a rainy day to visit. I know when we plan elaborate theme park trips, we typically will build in a day or two to adjust for weather and crowds and keep our schedule as flexible as possible to allow for adjustments if needed. Sometimes those extra days will be spent in different parks, while sometimes those extra days may be spent doing something completely different.

The real question is, if I purchase tickets online right now for May 1, 2016, and for some reason not able to attend on that day, do I completely lose the value of that admission? Is there a "change fee" that can be paid to visit on a different day, or if I'm too sick to venture out of my hotel on my reserved day am I S.O.L?

AJ Hummel: Honestly, I think people are interpreting this to be something different than what it really is. USH is not saying, "You must commit to a day in advance in order to visit," they are saying, "If you are willing and able to commit to a date in advance, we'll give you a discount." This is just an additional tool to help USH in estimating attendance and staffing appropriately, and the deals are the incentive for customers to go for it.

There are two things I would like to see, however, in order to avoid mass complaints:

1. The number of advance tickets is only a portion of the total available for that day (probably 1/2-2/3). If it was impossible to go to the park and purchase a ticket day-of, it could be a PR nightmare for USH after so many people were turned away.

2. If you decide you can't use your ticket on the scheduled day

BEFORE that date arrives, you can upgrade to the $95-anytime ticket by paying the difference. Although most people would probably be certain they can go before purchasing a date-specific ticket, it would be good to have a "just in case" option and fewer people trying to get refunds.

I'm becoming increasingly curious how everything is going to play out over the coming months. My guess is that USH is preparing for the worst case scenario and then will scale back restrictions later instead of adding restrictions as needed. Only time will tell whether this was the right approach.

Russell Meyer: You make some good points AJ. I think USH is only selling a relatively minor percentage (probably around a third) of the daily maximum capacity through this mechanism. However, by sweetening the pot with the early admission, it's almost imperative for any non-AP visitor to purchase the date-stamped tickets even though the monetary discount is not that much of an incentive. Buying a ticket at the gate is going to be a non-starter for serious fans during at least the first few months of WWoHP as the IOA opening showed with 6+ hour waits just to enter Hogsmeade, let alone to experience any of the attractions.

The other thing that worries me is that essentially the only way to get an admission discount is by reserving your day. You don't get any other discount for simply reserving online (like for USF/IOA), and I'm guessing there won't be any other discounts available (perhaps the discount through the City Pass will still exist…I do know that other City Passes can force you to lock in dates for certain attractions at the time of purchase). So if there's no reason to purchase a ticket in advance if you can't or are unwilling to lock in your date in advance, the lines at the park ticket windows are going to be insane.

It's clear USH is trying to avoid the debacle that occurred when WWoHP opened in Florida, but I think they're going a bit too far in trying to control people's visits. They've already restricted APs to the point that very few are buying (they tweaked the structure in the hopes of selling more), and now with this new policy, I wonder if they further depress what would have been a 6-month money machine once WWoHP opens.

Disney Moves to Seasonal Pricing for Theme Park Tickets
First published February 27, 2016

Walt Disney World and Disneyland made official this morning that their theme parks will start charging different prices for admission on different days of the year, starting tomorrow. The new seasonal pricing plan will create three pricing tiers for one-day theme park tickets: value, regular, and peak days. Disney will use its crowd calendars to assign days into one of the three price tiers, and single-day tickets now will be assigned to a specific day of use.

The upside is that the new plan will allow visitors who have the flexibility to visit on less crowded days to enjoy a lower-than-usual price for a single day's visit, as well as the smaller crowds in the park found on such days. The downside is that families with children in school likely will find it even more expensive to visit a Disney theme park, as many school vacation days likely will end up in the peak-days tier.

Of course, most visitors — especially to the Walt Disney World Resort — visit using multi-day tickets. Those tickets will not vary by tier but the prices on them will go up across the board tomorrow, as well.

One day, one-park tickets at Walt Disney World will cost $124 for peak days at the Magic Kingdom and $114 at Epcot, Animal Kingdom and Hollywood Studios. Regular days will cost $110 at the MK and $102 at the other parks. Prices for the value days will remain what they are now — $105 for the Magic Kingdom and $97 for the other three WDW parks.

One day, one-park tickets to Disneyland and Disney California Adventure will cost $119 for peak days, $105 for regular days, and $95 for value days. Those tickets currently cost $99 on all days of the year. There will be 83 value days remaining in 2016 — all weekdays during the school year. And there will be 83 peak days — during spring break, summer weekends and the holiday season in December.

Earlier this month, Universal Studios Hollywood adopted a dynamic discount system for one-day tickets bought in advance via the park's website. Universal kept the gate price of daily tickets the same for every day, but offers varying discounts based on the date you commit to visit.

The point of these variable, seasonal, dynamic pricing systems (whatever you wish to call them), is to provide another incentive for people to move their visits from busy days to less-busy ones. That allows the parks to better distribute their capital resources, as they no longer have to build excess capacity for peak periods that sits unused during less busy times.

In addition, peak pricing allows the parks to be more aggressive about admission increases, as these systems allow the park to avoid raising the price on less popular days, when people might not be inclined to visit at the higher prices.

Today's move leaves Universal Orlando's theme parks as the only ones among the nine most popular theme parks in the United States not to have some dynamic pricing system for its theme park tickets. [Editor's addition: Keep reading. You know what's coming next.] Earlier this month, Universal Orlando raised prices for its one-day and multi-day tickets, beating Disney to what's become the annual late-winter price increases for tickets at major theme parks.

Reader Poll: Will Variable Pricing Help 'Even Out' Crowd Levels at Disney?
It Won't Make a Difference: 75%
Yes, at Both Resorts: 12%
At Disneyland, but Not Disney World: 9%
At Disney World, but Not Disneyland: 4%

Readers respond:

AJ Hummel: In Florida, this isn't going to do anything. Very few people purchase one-day tickets at Walt Disney World, and those that do so are likely going to do so anyway.

In California, however, I think this may have an impact. While a lot of Disneyland visitors are either locals with APs or tourists visiting on multi-day tickets, there is still a sizable population that purchases one-day tickets. These may be people visiting with resident relatives who have APs, people who are visiting So Cal and just want to check out Disneyland for a day, or even just locals who only visit the park once or twice a year. For those that have flexibility, I think a $10-25 discount may be enough to persuade them to change the time of their visit. Low crowd days will probably get busier, and busy days will probably get a little more reasonable.

Note, however, that this will not reduce overall crowds or make major changes. In order to do that, Disneyland needs to completely revise their AP system. Personally, I'd like to see one of the following two alternatives put in place:

1. Keep AP levels as is, but significantly modify the payment plan. Instead of 12 payments, go with a 3 to 6 payment setup. Additionally, add an interest fee or similar to the payment plan to discourage people from using it.

2. Keep the Signature Plus AP, but get rid of all the other options. Instead of lower level APs, offer tickets with a set number of visits that can be used anytime in a 12 month period. Something like 5 visits for $300, 10 for $500, or 20 for $800 (with a flat $50-100 upcharge to enable park hopping on visits) would probably prove very popular. A payment plan could be offered for these tickets, but you would only be eligible to use the visits you have credit for. For example, if you bought a 10-visit ticket and had only paid off $300 worth of it, you would be suspended after six visits until more payments were made.

The variable pricing strategy Disney is switching to is not a bad idea, but I think more needs to be done before significant change can occur. I've got a feeling this will be coming over the next few years as it will be impossible to handle the Star Wars crowds on top of what is already present.

Universal Orlando Moves to Seasonal Pricing for Theme Park Tickets
First published May 31, 2016

The last major hold-out against seasonal pricing now has made the switch. Universal Orlando this week has started charging higher prices for its one-day theme park tickets, based on the time of year.

High-season pricing now is in effect for one-day tickets bought at the front gates of Universal Studios Florida and Islands of Adventure. One-day tickets bought at the gate now cost $119, up from the $105 that Universal had started charging in February. A one-day Park-to-Park ticket now sells for $169, up from $155.

The one-day ticket prices will fall back to their "normal" levels at the end of the summer vacation season, though we don't now for certain what those prices, or any potential low-season prices, might end up being. The prices for advance purchase and multi-day tickets remain the same as before and are not affected by one-day, front-gate seasonal pricing.

That makes Universal Orlando's approach different from sister park Universal Studios Hollywood. On the west coast, the $115 front gate price remains the same from day to day, while varying discounts of $10-20 a day are available for tickets bought in advance online, based on the date of your visit. Whether you are visiting Universal in Orlando or Los Angeles, however, the best way to get to the lowest price is to buy your tickets online in advance, where you can price your options without the pressure of making a decision while the family's waiting to get the park and you've got a crowd of impatient people in line behind you at the ticket booth.

The Disney theme parks also have adopted seasonal pricing, but Disney's daily one-day ticket price for a given date will be the same whether bought in advance online or in person at the park.

Who's Doing Date-Variable Pricing Better: Disney or Universal?
First published July 25, 2016

When Disney and Universal introduced date-variable pricing for one-day theme park tickets earlier this year, the two companies took different approaches. Disney assigned different prices to different days, setting one-day ticket prices at one of three levels based on estimated park attendance for those days, whether you bought your ticket in advance online or in person at the gate.

Universal Studios Hollywood, however, kept its front gate walk-up price the same for every day. Instead, Universal offered varying discounts off that price for people who bought their tickets in advance on universalstudioshollywood.com, based on the date of their planned visit. That not only allowed Universal to try to redistribute crowds to less crowded days — as Disney also is trying to do — it also created a financial incentive for fans to commit in advance to visiting on a certain date. At Disney, there's no such price incentive to buy in advance and commit to a date, as the price is the same in advance online as it is if you just walk up to the ticket booths on the day of your visit.

So how's that working out? This past weekend might have provided some insight.

Last weekend was a miserable time to be outside in Southern California. A now-30,000-acres-plus wildfire, burning just a few miles east of Six Flags Magic Mountain, darkened skies across the Los Angeles metropolitan area, dropping ash across many communities and making the whole town smell of smoke. And, by the way, did I mention that high temperatures on Saturday topped 100 degrees across much of the area?

And yet, Universal Studios Hollywood was packed all weekend.

The temperatures (and the smoke) weren't as bad down at Disneyland in Anaheim as they were up in Universal City, so it's not a true apples-to-apples comparison. But one has to wonder if so many people would have turned out at Universal over the weekend had some of them not committed to the dates by buying their discounted tickets in advance online. Neither Universal nor Disney report daily attendance, but wait times at the Disneyland parks seemed a tick or two less last weekend than the previous weekend, which offered better weather.

And, for what it's worth, various apps reported that wait times at Magic Mountain — which was much closer to the fire — were way below normal for the weekend, suggesting that crowds did bail on visiting the Six Flags park.

Weather affects theme park attendance at parks throughout the world. But the Orlando theme parks, which rely on out-of-town guests who commit to their visits sometimes months in advance, typically have been able to avoid weather-influenced swings in attendance, as people who've spent money to come to Central Florida to see the parks tend to show up, rain or shine.

Like at regional parks around the country, attendance at the Southern California theme parks is driven much more by locals than it is in Orlando. And locals can afford to be fickle about coming out the parks when the weather is less than ideal. But with its advance-purchase discount plan, has Universal Studios Hollywood found a way to bring some of that Orlando-style attendance resilience to Southern California?

That's another factor to consider as we continue to watch the effect of date-variable pricing on theme park attendance.

DISNEY MAKES ITS MOVE WITH MARVEL

One of the major ongoing stories in the theme park business over the past few years has been the issue of "what will Disney do with Marvel?" The comic book company's long-standing deal with Universal Studios prevents Disney from using almost all major Marvel characters, as well as the Marvel brand name, at the Walt Disney World Resort in Florida. There are no such restrictions at the Disneyland Resort in California, yet Disney's been slow to add any Marvel-themed attractions there.

Disney did announce its first Marvel-themed ride, a simulator-based Iron Man attraction, for Hong Kong Disneyland, but that ride had yet to open at the time this book went to press. But it was Disney's next move toward building a Marvel ride that set its fan base afire in 2016. How ironic that the decision to bring what might be its most popular current franchise to one of its U.S. theme parks would prove to be the single most unpopular thing that Disney did this year, at least among its most vocal fans.

Of course, as we sometimes do on Theme Park Insider, we went against the Disney fan conventional wisdom (if there is such as thing) and took an opposing view.

Why Guardians of the Galaxy is Better than The Twilight Zone for Disney's Tower of Terror
First published May 13, 2016

How in the world could Disney change the Twilight Zone Tower of Terror to a Guardians of the Galaxy Tower of Terror?

That's the question that many Disney fans are likely asking, as rumors intensify that Disney will in fact switch the theme of its Tower of Terror ride at Disney California Adventure (and perhaps even at Disney's Hollywood Studios in Florida) as early as late this year.

Let's start breaking down this question by noting that Disney already has installed a Tower of Terror ride without the Twilight Zone theme. At Tokyo DisneySea, the Tower of Terror is the former property of a character named Harrison Hightower, a member of the Society of Explorers and Adventurers who traveled the world collecting antiquities that he brought to keep in his tower hotel.

Ultimately, one of those treasures — the Shiriki Utundu idol — wasn't as inanimate as it seemed. After dispatching Hightower and cursing his hotel, the Shiriki Utundu has been sending visitors on a wild ride on the hotel's elevators — as revenge upon those who would disturb sacred relics.

Even if you've not read any of the rumors about the new Tower of Terror overlay, if you're familiar with Guardians of the Galaxy, perhaps that description of Harrison Hightower might sound familiar.

Here's the way that a Guardians overlay might not just work on Tower of Terror, but might even provide a better narrative device for the ride. Harrison Hightower's equivalent in the Guardians of the Galaxy franchise is Taneleer Tivan — a.k.a. the Collector. Featured briefly in the Guardians of the Galaxy movie, the Collector searches the galaxy gathering curiosities, including life forms, for his museum.

Disney could make a Guardians overlay work simply by starting with the Harrison Hightower framework for Tower of Terror and swapping the Collector in Hightower's place. Disney doesn't even need to change the exterior setting of the ride. It could remain the Hollywood Tower Hotel, while the story explains that Taneleer Tivan is using the property as cover for a secret new collection of stuff from our corner of the galaxy.

Why are we here? The Collector is trying to collect us, and it's up to the Guardians of the Galaxy to save us. We board the elevator, and the Collector tries to "file" us upstairs. But the Guardians attack, and we bounce up and down in middle of the battle before the Guardians prevail and we are freed.

Frankly, to me, that scenario provides a stronger narrative explaining what happens on the ride that the current Twilight Zone story does.

Here's some tough love for Tower of Terror fans. While I love the old shows, and I love the ride, Tower of Terror makes for a pretty weak episode of "The Twilight Zone." The best episodes illustrated ironic punishment: townspeople fearing aliens discovers that they are their own worst enemy, a woman whom other characters consider a hideous outcast is beautiful to us, a loner who just wants to get away from everyone to read books becomes the last person on Earth... and breaks his glasses.

The show wasn't really about the supernatural. It just used supernatural tropes to hold up a mirror to flawed human attitudes and behavior.

On Disney's Twilight Zone Tower of Terror, we visit an old Hollywood Hotel that's been hit by a freak lightning storm. Visitors disappeared in the strike, and now we're entering the decrepit remains of the hotel, only to fall under the influence of the weird forces that remain.

There's no irony. No statement about human behavior. Just a wild elevator ride in a fried building. You want irony? With its story of a sacred idol's revenge on a treasure hunter, Tokyo's Twilight Zone-free Tower of Terror does a better job of reflecting the spirit of an old episode of "The Twilight Zone" than Disney's Twilight Zone-themed Towers of Terror.

In my version of a perfect world, Disney just would bring the Harrison Hightower theme to the Tower of Terror at Disney California Adventure, including the spectacular preshow, which includes the best visual trick I've ever seen in person in a theme park (though videos of the Captain Jack transformation on the new Shanghai version of Pirates of the Caribbean suggest that might top it). Then Disney would build a Mystic Manor on the parking lot behind the Tower, and give us two pillars for an immersive Society of Explorers and Adventurers land.

But as much as I love SEA, it's nothing when compared with the popular support for Marvel. The use of the Collector seems to create an opportunity for a clever transition from DCA's Hollywood Land into a new immersive Marvel land that could be built behind the Tower. And even if a Marvel land is years away from happening, this proposed overlay creates an opportunity to refresh the Tower of Terror with a fun new narrative that works within both the existing ride and the Guardians franchise.

Disney hasn't confirmed its Guardians of the Galaxy Tower of Terror plans. But after thinking this through the context of what Disney did with the Tower in Tokyo, count me as cautiously optimistic.

Readers respond:

Rob McCullough: Dropping the Twilight Zone theme isn't as bothersome to me as I know it will be to some. This is because I know how amazing the story is at the TDS version featuring Harrison Hightower. I agree with Robert's take on the similarities of Hightower and the Collector. I like the idea of his using the HTH as his front for his collecting from Earth. The problem is most of the explanation for who Hightower was comes from murals painted on the walls of the lobby. You'd think if the Collector is hiding out in the hotel, there wouldn't be anything so obvious in the lobby setting up the story. How will the story be developed? Also, what would be our reason to go into such a derelict building in the first place? Come to think of it... why do we go into the two U.S. versions in the first place now? There is a real reason to visit in Tokyo. The Historical Society is hosting an open house to see the dilapidated hotel. Perhaps that's what it will be. Maybe the Collector has dispatched some of his minions to lure people into the HTH to see this historical landmark, "today only!" It still leaves some gaps in how the story of who he is left untold, at least in the lobby. Good or bad, real or hoax, it's going to be fun to see how this unfolds.

AJ Hummel: As far as the IP [intellectual property] goes, The Twilight Zone just isn't worth the licensing fees anymore. The current generation likely has limited familiarity with the IP and nobody rides the attraction because of the tie-in. Therefore, I support changing the ride to a different IP or, as Robert proposed, removing the IP entirely and going with the Hightower theme. The reality is, however, that Disney wants Marvel and that Marvel would draw way more visitors than Hightower or Mystic Manor, so like it or not, Marvel it is.

My main concern with the Guardians of the Galaxy idea is that it feels cheap, contrived, and solely to cash in on a currently popular IP that has unknown staying power. The Collector is a character who was in two (or maybe three) scenes in Guardians of the Galaxy and will not be involved in the sequel. If you set the ride in his mansion (the current plan from what I've heard), it makes no sense because his mansion is on Knowhere, not Earth (which is where the rest of Marvel Land will be). If you want to keep the hotel and make it the Collector's Earth base, that also causes problems because you've then got to explain why he has an Earth base and explain why we are going to visit him. You've then got to make the ride convincing, and it's pretty difficult to imagine a way to fit a high-speed elevator into the Guardians of the Galaxy universe. The best thing I can think of would be doing something related to the Kyln Escape sequence, but that's got problems as well.

My hope is that Disney will announce this and receive enough negative reactions that they decide to go back to the drawing board and come up with something better. Without spending hours writing a Theme Park Apprentice type proposal, here's just one idea: Retheme the ride to Stark Tower Hollywood. Guests have been invited by Tony Stark to test his latest invention: A teleportation device based on the energy of the Space Stone that can be used to evacuate an area rapidly in the event of a catastrophe. In the preshow, Stark appears via video conference from the original Stark Tower in New York and briefs testers on his device, telling them that he will be transporting them across the country and warning that they may experience some strange gravitational shifts during the journey. Once guests board the test vehicle, the ride backs into the elevator shaft and then swirling light occurs during the initial rapid ascent, with the first show scene opening to show an animatronic Stark in his laboratory. However, Thanos shows up and takes the Space Stone, then uses the power of the Infinity Gauntlet to send testers to several different locations (possibly Wakanda, Asgard, and deep space to maximize character cameos). The climax of the ride occurs when riders view the Disneyland Resort from the top of the tower and a scrim over the opening makes it appear as if the Avengers are fighting Thanos above the park. They succeed in knocking the Space Stone from Thanos's gauntlet, which sends riders plunging all the way down the tower and returning to their point of origin at Stark Tower Hollywood.

Whatever Disney ends up doing, I'll wait until I ride the final attraction before passing judgment on it. However, I just have a hard time thinking a Guardians of the Galaxy redo can be equivalent or better than what we have now, both in terms of quality and popularity. The current proposal sounds a little too much like, say, retheming Splash Mountain to the Adventures of Mr. Big...it has an IP tie-in and could possibly work, but there are just so many better options.

Let's back up a bit and revisit our first look at Mr. Harrison Hightower, to understand better why his story offers a nice fit with the Tower of Terror ride.

Who is Disney's Harrison Hightower?
First published May 23, 2012

In just a couple weeks, we'll be getting our first look at the completed changes underway at Disney California Adventure. Disney's poured $1 billion into the changes and additions at the Disneyland Resort's second gate, and the glimpses we've seen so far have been dazzling.

But in a few years, when Buena Vista Street and Cars Land have grown familiar and Disney's looking for something else to do to add a little more spark to DCA, I hope that they'll think about giving Harrison Hightower a call.

Who is Harrison Hightower?

World traveller. Real estate developer. Collector of rare antiques and antiquities. Billionaire. Celebrity.

And, oh yeah, completely fictional.

Harrison Hightower is the protagonist in Tokyo DisneySea's version of Tower of Terror. Without a Twilight Zone overlay for the ride in Japan, Disney's Imagineers concocted Mr. Hightower (get it?), the wealthy, vain, and egomaniacal (not necessarily in that order) developer who built the Hotel Hightower at the corner of Broadway and Park Avenue in New York. (Look at a map of Manhattan for the joke.)

And, I hope, one day he will become the proprietor of Disney California Adventure's Tower of Terror, as well.

Why? Because California Adventure's Tower of Terror, while great fun, isn't as good an attraction as the original in Florida, which Theme Park Insider readers consistently rate among the very best in the world for its wild ride of random drops and special effects. If Disney isn't about to spend tens of millions of dollars to improve the DCA ToT's ride to that level, it could, with much less expense, improve its story.

I love The Twilight Zone. The best episodes of Rod Serling's anthology series from the 1960s brilliantly illustrated irony in the human existence, often using the supernatural to place in sharp relief our very natural, human flaws. No one believes the crazy man on the airplane, even though he turns out to be the only one who's right. A selfish man wishes away all of mankind so he can read in peace, only to be left with no one to repair his eyeglasses after a holocaust. Invaders hold back, allowing the residents of Maple Street turn on each other out of fear and eventually do themselves in.

Disney did amazing work to craft a video introduction for the Florida and California Tower of Terror attractions. Smart video editing allows Serling himself (long dead at the time of the ride's development) to set up the story, which involves a lightning strike sending visitors at the Hollywood Tower Hotel into the Twilight Zone.

But something's missing: the irony. Why are these nameless guests destined for oblivion? What did they do to deserve or enable what ought to be a deliciously ironic punishment? Heck, who are these people, anyway? We never get to meet any of them. Without any emotional stakes, we're left with the supernatural gimmickry of the Twilight Zone, without the human insight that made the series so special.

In Tokyo, we instead get the story of one Harrison Hightower, a pompous man who's returned to America with his greatest prize, the Shiriki Utundu idol from Africa.

To the natives, Shiriki Utundu is no mere idol. He is their god - an angry god, ready to curse whomever takes him from his people. Hightower, being the arrogant man he is, will have no such silliness, and he invites the press to a party where he will show off his new prize.

But on "that fateful night," Shiriki Utundu has his revenge. In an amazing pre-show, we learn Harrison Hightower's fate, then are ushered into the hotel's elevators to see the outcome for ourselves. As we ascend, we see Shiriki Utundu deliver Harrison Hightower to his fate before turning to face us, to ensure that we get the message: Don't mess with Shiriki Utundu.

Harrison Hightower paid for his sins of arrogance, excess, and hubris. The prize he thought would validate him became his undoing. The ironic punishment is served.

Rod Serling would approve.

So, perhaps, we've found our irony, after all: Disney best expresses the spirit of The Twilight Zone in the one Tower of Terror that never mentions its name.

Disney Makes Guardians/Tower of Terror Switch Official
First published July 23, 2016

Disney and Marvel this afternoon made official that Guardians of the Galaxy will replace The Twilight Zone Tower of Terror at Disney California Adventure.

Marvel Studios President Kevin Feige made the announcement during Marvel's presentation at the San Diego Comic-Con today, with Disney following up by posting a promotional video with Imagineer Joe Rohde to the official Disney Parks Blog. The Tower of Terror will close early next year for its transformation into Guardians of the Galaxy - Mission: Breakout!

The storyline for the new attraction matches what I wrote here on Theme Park Insider in May. Essentially, Disney is taking the Tokyo DisneySea storyline for that Tower of Terror (which does not include "The Twilight Zone"), and swapping The Collector (Taneleer Tivan) for Harrison Hightower and Rocket Raccoon for the Shiriki Utundu.

As Rohde explained, "the setting is a kind of fortress that's owned by the mysterious Collector and it's packed with creatures and his latest acquisitions from across the universe. Now he has imprisoned the Guardians of the Galaxy and they're hanging in display cases over a giant abyss. The captor doesn't know it but

Rocket Raccoon has escaped and is enlisting our aid... to help the Guardians in a breakout scheme."

Disney won't be changing the physical structure of the ride, but it will be adding random drop profiles as on Florida's Tower of Terror, which will retain its Twilight Zone theme. Disney also will add music from the Guardians soundtrack to the ride, but if Disney also brings over the Pepper's Ghost effect in DisneySea's Tower preshow for this Guardians of the Galaxy attraction, that alone could help make this new version of the drop ride a hit.

Of course, anything Marvel starts with a huge reservoir of goodwill among fans. Feige said that the new Guardians ride will be Disney's first step in creating a Marvel-themed land in Disney California Adventure. Guardians of the Galaxy - Mission: Breakout will open next summer.

Readers respond:

Randy Keith: Awful idea. It doesn't matter if The Twilight Zone is still relevant or not, the ride stands on its own. And no matter what they do to it, Tower of Terror is too unique to just turn it to something else. They should just demolish it and create a new ride from scratch, or better yet forget about it. It's too bad Disney would rather get rid of a ride that is popular just because it's not based on a recent hit.

Tony Perkins: I'd rather Disney just demolished ToT and built a new ride instead. I like ToT. I didn't love it. But this reskinning seems like a big step backward. Robert, I think you're wrong on this one. We'll see...

O T: I read Robert's article about why Guardians would be a better fit, and although he made a great case I always felt the falling elevator was a perfect fit for the theme. I love the Guardian film a lot (maybe because it has no super heroes in it) but it needed it's own ride from scratch. Joe Rohde is trying to hard to sell it [but] calling it a new addition to the park when you take away a classic is using the wrong words.

AJ Hummel: Sometimes, I really hate being right. While I'm not dead set against this change, I must admit that the video didn't exactly make me feel excited for the new version of the attraction. I'm a huge fan of Guardians of the Galaxy and I would love to see them get a theme park attraction, but I feel like the results will be subpar due to adapting the IP onto an attraction that isn't the best suited for the IP. (I still say Avengers Tower would have been the proper Marvel retheme.) The current version of the ride is one of the few I would consider perfect, and I do hope that near perfection can be achieved again. If not, I'll probably take a break from Disney for a couple years and go enjoy Justice League and Harry Potter one county north.

I am curious, however, if Disney has a contingency plan in place should this attraction flop. While it can be difficult to predict, I seriously think that a poor redo of this ride could break the AP bubble that currently supports the Disneyland Resort. Even the loss of Aladdin did not cause the level of negativity I'm seeing around the internet now. That makes me question this: If Mission: Breakout fails, does that ruin the future of Marvel attractions?

David Brown: When are Disney 'fans' going to get it into their heads that Disney don't make attractions for them - they make attractions for Joe Public who just want to be entertained and don't care how so long as they enjoy themselves?

As Robert says, this is a good fit and I suspect the crowds will love it. Disney are a business and they exist to make money and entertain people. If their fans like it then all to the good but the fans don't drive decisions.

From an anonymous reader: Why did Disney invest a billion dollars perfecting California Adventure, if they were just going to turn around and ruin it? Three classic attractions ripped out in one year: Aladdin, Soarin' Over California and now Twilight Zone. There is no reason ever to go back to California Adventure. Sure the scenery is pretty, but beautiful scenery can be enjoyed all over California, and for a lot less money.

Blake Meredith: Ho, boy. I really thought this was a total long shot and never gave the rumors much precedence. I am pretty pessimistic about this change, but final results will determine if this is for the best or not. What really upsets me is the total disregard for the supposed overall theme of the park. At least with the ToT, we had a distinctly Hollywood attraction, which, in a park supposedly themed to California, fit perfectly. Now we're getting a futuristic, sci-fi building in the middle of the Hollywood backlot. Walt is rolling in his grave. If Disney was so concerned with The Twilight Zone rights, they could have EASILY copy-pasted the Tokyo version, with slight adjustments to ensure they keep their clause with the Tokyo Land Company intact. Just a totally botched opportunity, IMO.

Now, on the plus side, Walt Disney Imagineering has their top dogs working on this project. Rohde is arguably the best Imagineer since [Tony] Baxter, and the team around him is top-notch as well. If the pre-show experience is even close to the Tokyo version, this will be a great experience. On to the broader picture, I think WDI has pretty much confirmed the development of the long rumored Marvel Land expansion coming to DCA, which, on the whole, is great news. I'm going to project an announcement of the project after the completion of Star Wars Land, so we probably won't see any ground-breaking on further expansion until 2020 at the earliest.

Disneyobsession: Another AWFUL decision forced onto Team Disney Anaheim by the Walt Disney Company. When will this end? Tower of Terror is a DCA classic. It has a huge fan base, an original story line, and a great theme. Although it may just be a scaled down version of the Orlando ride, it's nevertheless still among the top 10 greatest rides that Disney ever built. Unfortunately, by tearing down such a beloved ride, WDC has basically just slapped all Disney fans in the face. The reaction from all DLR fans from across the globe has been overwhelmingly negative. It sheds a bad light on the company and will cause a PR nightmare for WDC. Sad to say it, but WDC is literally run by complete idiots. What scares me is the fact that WDC is willing to just tear down fan favorites and replace them with something that the fan base has clearly showed resentment for. I mean what's next... Re-theming Haunted Mansion to "Halloweentown the Ride"... Changing POTC to "The Battle of Jack Sparrow"... Or changing Matterhorn to "Frozen: Elsa's Magical Journey"? I mean where does the IP madness stop? With all of these moronic decisions, it's not surprising that Hong Kong Disneyland is failing, Disneyland Paris is failing, Walt Disney Studios Park is failing, Shanghai Disney's attendance is below WDC's forecasts, WDW is experiencing declining revenue and attendance, and now the DLR is also experiencing declining attendance. You can only piss off fans for so long before they finally reach their tipping point. I know I have. After having been a die-hard Disney fan for almost my entire life, I can now say that I resent the company and everything that it stands for. Iger is an idiot and should have been fired ages ago. [Bob] Chapek is also an idiot and should be demoted immediately. So yeah, goodbye Disney you just lost one of your most loyal fans. I just hope other devoted Disney fans follow my lead and boycott the parks until Iger is fired.

Ben Mills: Let's remember that Paris' version (which is a carbon copy of DCA's) isn't likely to change any time soon. So it'll still be out there somewhere in the world. Personally, I'm on Team-Totally-Okay-With-This, so long as Orlando's stays intact. Like Robert says, it could actually end up being a better fit, particularly if it anchors a new land. I love variety between parks, rather than straight clones, so long as it's done well.

And judging from the artwork, that building has the potential to look stunning at night. I hope they don't use Rock n Roller Coaster as the model for whatever coaster they work into the eventual Marvel Land though. Let's take the TRON design and turn it into a Black Widow motorcycle ride, yeah?

From an anonymous reader: Sometimes we think one dimensionally. WDC already has committed to converting the majority of the Hollywood Pictures backlot into Marvel. We are not privy to the plans. But, our consistent questioning is well placed.

But, an answer will not be known for sometime. DCA, as it's now called, is still suffering from a lack of E-Ticket attractions that generate excitement that translates into admissions that translates into revenue. Over the next decade DCA will dramatically evolve. And we will cherish the new E-Tickets just like we cherished everything that's been added to Disneyland POST Walt.

And remember... the DCA version of TofT has always been TRASHED when compared to WDW. And rightfully so!

So What is Really Happening with Epcot?
First published July 17, 2016

Over the past few weeks, the rumor mill's been working overtime churning out wild stories about what's happening next with Epcot at the Walt Disney World Resort.

Guardians of the Galaxy is taking over Mission Space. Guardians of the Galaxy is taking over the Energy pavilion. Tron Lightcycle Coaster is taking over Test Track. Tron Lightcycle Coaster is taking over the old Wonders of Life pavilion. [Insert Pixar property here] is taking over the Imagination pavilion.

After introducing Frozen to the Norway pavilion, it's a simple exercise for Disney fans to match the remaining World Showcase pavilions with recent Disney animation franchises set in those countries... or someplace that could pass for those countries.

Heck, for Disney fans, playing the Epcot rumor game is as much a pastime as playing Pokemon Go. Pick a rumor — or make one up! — then throw it up on Reddit for karma, your blog for page views, Facebook for likes, or Twitter for retweets. And if you're a real pro at the game, you probably do all those.

But what if you're not into playing games but just want to plan a family theme park vacation? What if you just want to know what's really going to happen with Epcot?

Here's the not-so-secret scoop: Something will happen, but

probably not for a while. So it's not worth holding off on a Walt Disney World visit to wait for the next big change at Epcot. Besides, Disney World's got plenty of new stuff coming in the next few years at its other theme parks.

Which is why we believe that Epcot will have to wait its turn for any big new additions or changes. The park did get a couple of significant changes for this summer, after all. Soarin' got its third theater and a new show. And, as we mentioned, the Norway pavilion got that Frozen overhaul, with Maelstrom becoming Frozen Ever After, and the Royal Sommerhus meet-and-greet providing a new home for Anna and Elsa.

If you look at the current decade, the Magic Kingdom got its big project with New Fantasyland, which opened in phases between 2012 and 2014. Disney's Animal Kingdom is the midst of its big project, with its nighttime expansion starting next year and Pandora The World of Avatar opening in 2017. Disney's Hollywood Studios is next after that, with Toy Story Land and Star Wars Land under development, as well as new a new parking lot entry and exit.

So that leaves Epcot.

At this stage, it appears that Walt Disney Imagineering is spitballing ideas for how to refresh Epcot, with the expectation that major construction will begin at Epcot once Star Wars Land is nearing completion at Disney's Hollywood Studios. Disney would like to have a steady stream of major new projects at Walt Disney World to promote over the next decade, so that the resort isn't caught out with no new rides for years in a row, as it was in the years before the New Fantasyland project. A couple big Epcot projects would fit nicely on that schedule after the new lands open at Disney's Hollywood Studios.

That timeline gives Imagineering a year or two to firm up plans for what those projects will be. During that time, leaks from Imagineering HQ in Glendale, Calif. will keeping prompting "telephone" games that eventually make their way into Internet rumors. That said, though, Disney's been establishing some patterns with its recent theme park projects, and until we see some evidence otherwise, we should expect those patterns to continue at Epcot.

Most importantly among those, Disney now seems focused on promoting and extending its film franchises when developing new theme park attractions in the United States. So it's hard to imagine Disney breaking that pattern by developing new non-fiction attractions not tied to an existing Disney franchise or developing anything based on original fictional IP. Bringing Frozen to Norway wasn't a one-off. It's the future of Epcot, barring the Disney board picking a successor to CEO Bob Iger who decides to switch course from Iger's franchise-focused strategy for the company.

Fat chance of that happening.

Also, Disney has shown that it is willing to invest the money to build new attractions from scratch, instead of relying solely on overlays and refurbishments of existing attractions. Frozen-style overlays are the solution when Disney feels like it needs to get something into the parks fast. But for big Epcot projects following the DHS lands, expect new construction — most likely following the demolition of some existing pavilion or pavilions.

That doesn't mean we might not see another franchise overlay before that, though. Think of the timeline again. Pandora's coming next year to Animal Kingdom. But if Toy Story Land isn't going to be ready for 2018, it's conceivable that Disney would decide to drop another Frozen-style overlay in Epcot to fill the gap between Pandora and Toy Story Land for its 2018 promotions. That decision would need to come by the end of the year, so WDI would need to be ready within the next couple of months to move a plan from the spitball stage to actual blueprints. But remember that those plans might never actually come to development, should Disney end up feeling comfortable that Toy Story Land will be ready by 2018.

Then we start the same process in anticipation of Star Wars Land being ready for 2019, or not. Again, if that construction is good to go, there's no need for an overlay. If not... well, maybe there would be.

Assuming all goes well for the two new lands at DHS and they meet their (as yet publicly unannounced) construction deadlines, we are looking at 2020 — at the earliest — for any major new construction projects at Epcot. And it's entirely possible that Disney will choose to give Star Wars Land a couple of years to carry the promotional burden for the resort before moving ahead with any major new capital project. That puts new Epcot projects off until 2021, or until the park's 40th anniversary in 2022.

So there's your context. If things are not moving as planned over at Hollywood Studios, Epcot might be getting a franchise-based overlay of an existing pavilion in 2018 or 2019. But if the DHS lands are opening in those years, some entirely new pavilion or pavilions likely will be replacing an existing Epcot pavilion or pavilions in 2020 or beyond.

And all of this is off the table, of course, if the economy tanks or international tourism to Central Florida continues to decline. But if tourists keeping coming down to Orlando, Disney fans should expect something new at Epcot within the next few years. We just don't know exactly what yet. And, we suspect, neither does Disney.

Readers respond:

B Goodwin: I hold faith that, if the right amount of time and thought goes into an overhaul of Epcot, that Disney goes back to the basics, and re-establishes itself to the founding principles of the park. I get that Disney DESPERATELY needed to get a Frozen ride out quickly, and don't resent the Norway overlay too much. And new rides in World Showcase (which it really, really needs) based on country-specific Disney IP is fine, as long as the food, exhibits, and architecture (and beer) strive to stay true to the local spirit of their countries. A couple of well-done new countries could go a long way to increase ticket sales, too.

But please go back to basics for Future World. Take your inspiration from the human spirit for innovation and exploration - not Disney movie characters thrown in for toy sales on the way out of the ride. Living Seas barely gets a pass, because the aquarium is still fun to look at, and there's lots of educational exhibits to explore once you get done Finding Nemo.

But if you are going to replace Ellen's Energy Adventure (please!), then make it something educational and fun. And if Rocket Raccoon has to replace Gary Sinise at Mission Space, that's fine too - but keep it focused on the human desire to reach for the stars. A bit of stunt casting is fine, but I don't need to go in Groot's salad spinner for the sake of going on it.

And the characters of Pixar taking you on a walk through your imagination is a great idea (bring Figment along too, please), as long as the focus of the ride is Imagination, not toys on the way out through the gift shop.

PLEASE return to the basic principles that made the park the third busiest in North America, and my favorite. Not some flashy, quick, attention getting, lowest denominator settling, place to go on rides that make you giggle.

Can Walt Disney World Really Make a Guardians of the Galaxy Theme Park Ride?
First published August 20, 2016

Is a Guardians of the Galaxy roller coaster about to replace Ellen's Energy Adventure at Walt Disney World's Epcot? Will the Guardians of the Galaxy characters appear in the upcoming Avengers: Infinity War movie?

These might seem like somewhat unrelated questions. Sure, they both involve Marvel's Guardians of the Galaxy franchise. But one is about a theme park ride and the other a movie. Yet the two questions are intimately related, and could have profound legal consequences for the Walt Disney Company and its parks.

Let's catch up. Actor Vin Diesel, who voices Groot in the Guardians of the Galaxy, spilled on Facebook this week that the Guardians characters would be appearing in the upcoming

Avengers film, which opens in 2018. Disney-owned Marvel takes an aggressive approach toward connecting its characters in the Marvel Cinematic Universe, so the slip didn't blow anyone away with shock.

So what does this have to do with theme parks? As any long-time Theme Park Insider reader knows, Universal Studios back in the 1990s secured the theme park rights to Marvel characters for Universal Orlando. For a while, it even had the global rights to use Marvel in its theme parks. Those rights have elapsed, but they remain in the Japan market for the next several years, and in perpetuity in Orlando. That deal, which you can read on the U.S. Securities and Exchange Commission website, effectively prohibits Disney from using most Marvel characters, or even the word "Marvel," inside the theme parks of the Walt Disney World Resort.

Notice that I wrote "most." The contract, which Marvel signed long before Disney acquired it, prohibits other theme parks from using the characters that Universal does, along with any other members of those characters families and their associated villains. If you speak legalese, here is the relevant subsection of the contract, IV.B.1.a.1.i. (Note that MCA was Universal's parent company at the time, which is why it's mentioned as a party in the deal.)

East of The Mississippi - any other theme park is limited to using characters not currently being used by MCA at the time such other license is granted. [For purpose of this subsection and subsection iv, a character is "being used by MCA" if (x) it or another character of the same "family" (e.g., any member of THE FANTASTIC FOUR, THE AVENGERS or villains associated with a hero being used) is more than an incidental element of an attraction, is presented as a costumed character, or is more than an incidental element of the theming of a retail store or food facility; and, (y) in addition, if such character or another character from the same "family" is an element in any MCA marketing during the previous year. Any character who is only used as a costume character will not be considered to be "being used by MCA" unless it appears as more than an incidental element in MCA's marketing.]

The question of what constitutes membership in a character "family" is key here. The contract explicitly references the Avengers, which are represented at Islands of Adventure in the Incredible Hulk Coaster. That provision prohibits Walt Disney World, or any other theme park east of the Mississippi, from using any of the characters in the Avengers family, or the villains fighting them, in their theme parks.

But does an appearance in an Avengers film constitute making the Guardians of the Galaxy members of the Avengers "family"? That is literally a multi-million dollar question for the Walt Disney Company. One could make a common-sense argument that a visiting a family isn't the same as being adopted by it. But this is contract law, where what's written on the page rules over whatever logical argument one might try to make. If Disney were to go ahead and develop a Guardians-themed attraction at Disney World, then put those characters in an Avengers film, Universal owner Comcast could sue Marvel for breach of contract, arguing that by appearing the Avengers film, the Guardians have effectively become members of that family.

If a judge or jury buys that argument, Disney World would have to close that attraction, remove all Guardians branding from the Disney World parks and all of its promotional material (every guidemap, billboard, and ad... anywhere) and potentially have to pay Comcast many millions of dollars in damages.

I cannot imagine any lawyer allowing Disney to take that risk.

So either Disney needs to:

- cut a deal with Comcast in which Comcast would acknowledge that the Guardians are not members of the Avengers family and agrees not to take action against Disney for developing a Guardians attraction in Florida, or
- keep the Guardians completely segregated from Universal Orlando's Marvel characters on the screen and in the books, or

- forget about using the Guardians at Disney World after Infinity War comes out.

I also can't imagine that Comcast would agree to the option 1 deal with Disney as nothing more than a corporate favor. Comcast and NBCUniversal would need to get something from Disney in return (a la the Oswald the Lucky Rabbit/Al Michaels deal). That's why we take any Guardians-related rumor for Disney World with a Gibraltar-sized grain of salt.

Whatever the outcome, though, we know this — some lawyers are keeping busy.

VIRTUAL REALITY IN THE PARKS

Virtual reality has been around for years. But 2016 brought the first large-scale implementation of VR in theme park attractions in the United States, as Six Flags added VR to several of its roller coasters across the country. That led to VR experimentation by Cedar Point on one of its coasters, and SeaWorld's announcement that it would add VR to its Kraken roller coaster in Orlando for 2017. Germany's Europa Park started the trend in late 2015, followed by Universal Studios Japan in January 2016. While many fans expressed skepticism about wearing a VR headset on a coaster, many of the fans who actually tried it loved it, and designers seem eager to add VR and augmented reality technology to their tool set in creating new themed experiences.

Six Flags to Add Virtual Reality to Nine Coasters This Year
First published March 3, 2016

Six Flags announced this morning that it will add virtual reality headsets on nine of its roller coasters across the country this year — and some will have limited interactive game play.

The New Revolution coaster at Six Flags Magic Mountain, which was undergoing renovations to celebrate its 40th anniversary as the world's first steel looping coaster, will get a storyline where riders are piloting fighter jets in a battle against alien invaders. From Six Flags' announcement:

Taking in the view around them, riders will see other aircraft in an underground secret bunker. As the aircraft moves to a landing pad, it begins to launch its thruster engines, lifting the craft straight up through the roof. During the ascent, riders can test fire their weapons using the world's first-ever interactive gameplay technology on a roller coaster. As riders clear the roof, they realize they are on top of a skyscraper and about to launch off the edge of the building diving straight down on the first drop of the ride. The aircraft races through the city until reaching the edge of the skyline where riders see the mother ship hovering above. The mother ship is heavily protected by drones and the mission is to get past the drones, fire on the mother ship and destroy it.

The New Revolution will open to season passholders for a sneak preview on March 26. The alien invasion story line also will appear on five other coasters:

- Shock Wave at Six Flags Over Texas in Arlington, opening March 10 for sneak preview
- Dare Devil Dive at Six Flags Over Georgia, opening March 12 for sneak preview
- Ninja at Six Flags St. Louis
- Steamin' Demon at The Great Escape
- Goliath at La Ronde

In addition, Six Flags is adding VR to three of its Superman roller coasters. In this story line...

[Riders] will be fully immersed in the 360-degree comic-book world of Metropolis. Guests will be taken on a leisurely (or so they think) tour of the city of Metropolis, courtesy of Lex Corp Sky Tours. Just after departing the station riders encounter Lex Luthor who uses an anti-gravity gun along with his army of Lex Bots to create chaos

throughout the city with cars, taxis and buses floating in mid-air around the rider's vehicle. As the Lexbots continue shooting at the vehicle, Superman uses heat vision to destroy the anti-gravity gun, causing all objects to suddenly fall, including the train as it takes the first giant drop of the roller coaster. Riders then soar alongside Superman as he battles the evil Lexbots through hairpin twists and turns, loops, dips and dives before ultimately defeating Lex and the Lexbots, and returning safely back into the station.

The three participating coasters will be:

- Superman Krypton Coaster at Six Flags Fiesta Texas
- Superman The Ride at Six Flags New England
- Superman Ride of Steel at Six Flags America

On all nine coasters, riders will wear Samsung Gear VR powered by Oculus headsets. The nine will be the first virtual reality coasters in North America, according to Six Flags.

Reality Check: Six Flags Revolutionizes Coasters with VR
First published March 25, 2016

The idea sounds ridiculous, we know.

Strapping a virtual reality headset to your face while riding a roller coaster? That's just crazy talk. For years, we've been telling people to keep their eyes open and to watch the track when they ride a coaster. That provides the visual cue your brain needs to help your body prepare for the drops, twists, airtime, and turns it will encounter on these high-speed thrill rides.

Yeah, people ride coasters in the dark. Or backwards. For some, not having that visual cue amplifies the thrill. But it's one thing to deny yourself a look at what's coming on the ride ahead. It's something else entirely to replace what you see with an alternate reality.

That's when so many fans who haven't experienced a virtual

reality coaster turn green and start looking around for the nearest barf bag. But having ridden Six Flags' The New Revolution this morning, allow me to tell you this:

Forget everything you fear about virtual reality roller coasters. Wearing a VR headset on a roller coaster isn't a nauseating experience.

It's a liberating one.

To celebrate the 40th anniversary of the world's first steel vertical looping coaster, Six Flags Magic Mountain has transformed Revolution into The New Revolution, installing new trains with more comfortable restraints, repainting the track, and... oh yeah, offering Samsung Gear VR powered by Oculus headsets to all riders age 13 and older, at no extra charge.

Wearing the headset completely changes the experience of riding The New Revolution. No longer do you see and feel yourself riding this iconic coaster across a wooded hillside near Magic Mountain's front gate. Now, you're strapped into a single-seat fighter jet, battling aliens in an Independence Day-like dogfight to save the planet.

Nausea? Nope. The VR footage you watch synchs with the action of flying across the coaster's track. You simply feel as if you are experiencing the most life-like video game ever. I've yet to ride on a shaker seat or flight simulator that truly recreates the physical sensation of dropping more than 100 feet, looping through an inversion, and feeling the wind rush by at 55 miles per hour as you fly through one turn after another. You feel all that here, on a real coaster.

And yet... you don't see how far you are above the ground. You don't see the loop or the tunnel coming. You just see the action on the screen in front you, comfortably secured to your face by four padded Velcro straps. And with these new trains, you feel the physical ride much more smoothly than you ever would on any of those "jiggle box" (as my wife calls them) simulator attractions.

If there's a knock to be made on the ride by thrill fans it's that this doesn't really feel like you're riding a roller coaster. While you still feel those same physical sensations, changing the visual experience transforms The New Revolution into a different type of attraction. It's not a roller coaster. It's not a simulator. It's the best of both things — the real experience of riding a coaster with the storytelling capabilities of a simulator ride.

If you've been wondering when the theme park industry would develop a fresh, new type of ride — it's here. Many of us have fallen into the habit of always looking to Disney and Universal for industry advances. But after enjoying Six Flags' Theme Park Insider Award-winning Justice League Battle for Metropolis last year, which melded interactive gameplay with a 3D motion-base ride, and experiencing The New Revolution this year, here's a crazy idea — the biggest innovator in theme parks today might just be Six Flags.

Readers respond:

From an anonymous reader: I think it's awesome tech and would be willing to give it a shot. Very cool of you to report on this Robert! That said, there are two pretty major downsides I can see on this:

One is being handed this headset in July when it's 102 degrees and after about 100,000 people have put it on before me. Just sitting in the seat sometimes behind someone in a wife beater can be wet and disgusting, I can't imagine strapping something on my face totally soaked in sweat and sunscreen will be enjoyable.

And two, not a fan on not being able to see the other riders and what they may attempt to do. If/when one of these comes off it's a pretty serious projectile, but I am referring more to loose items flying out. We know that people ruined the dueling aspect of Universal Orlando's Dueling Dragons [now Dragon Challenge] by throwing stuff (and blinding a guy for life), I have to think the temptation for some to spit or throw things would be increased if they think they can get away with it.

I have been splashed before by bugs, spit, vomit, and hope-to-God-it-was-just-water intentionally and unintentionally on night rides where people did stuff like this. I'm not a neat freak, just aware of things bodily fluids can (and do!) transmit.

Robert Niles: I felt better riding the coaster today than I felt just sitting in a chair and watching the VR video at Magic Mountain last month. Back then, the disconnect between seeing motion on the VR screen and not feeling it in "real life" gave me twinge of green at a couple spots. But today, because I was feeling the motion suggested on the screen, I felt completely comfortable and at ease during the ride. The experience made me wonder if a VR coaster would feel more comfortable than stationary VR - again, because there no longer is that disconnect between what you are seeing and what you are feeling.

As for sanitation, Six Flags has people spraying the units with disinfectant between rides. And they've got hundreds of these headgear sets. We'll know how the experience is in July when we get there, but at least Six Flags appears to have anticipated the problems and objections with the headgear and is trying (at this point) to alleviate them.

England's Alton Towers converted its Air roller coaster to the VR Galactica the day before The New Revolution opened at Six Flags. Our reader Ben Mills was there to cover for us.

Ben Mills: I rode Galactica on Thursday morning. (And again on Thursday afternoon, and again on Friday morning - which should tell you how I felt about it.)

I've been working professionally with VR quite a bit over the last year and, of everything I've experienced, Galactica is one of the best examples of what the medium can do. It's about as far away from a slapped-on gimmick as can be imagined - the designers have started from a place of understanding what makes Air (which has been plussed onto Galactica) work, and built a VR experience from there.

And I'd entirely echo Robert's thoughts about nausea. Air is admittedly a much smoother and more relaxing ride than most coasters to begin with, but VR actively *improves* the experience. I felt no queasiness whatsoever. If anything, well-crafted VR helps your brain process what's happening physically. VR creators have been exploring how to create experiences that work with the viewer being generally static, but a coaster offers freedom from that constraint.

On a more standard theme park note, the thing I'd celebrate most about Galactica is that it does what we've been asking for from theme park attractions for a while - it builds an experience around the joy of discovery rather than resorting to yet another generic fight/battle story. While it deploys a number of sci-fi tropes and a 'and then something goes wrong...' plot point, it does so with real joy - it's all about exploring new frontiers, more The Martian than Star Wars.

Oh, one more thought - Galactica whips you from one scenario to another, through the plot device of wormholes. You take in a launch pad, a space station, an icy tundra and a Mars-esque lava pit on your journey.

Interestingly, the one environment that I didn't find myself believing in was the last of those. VR (done well) is generally brilliant at convincing the brain it is experiencing what it is seeing. But it was just a jump too far for me to correlate the visuals of a hot environment with the feeling of rushing through the sky on a cold English morning.

I suppose that's a compromise designers will face when adapting existing rides into VR experiences. It'll be interesting to see whether Merlin can take things to the next level for Ghost Train at Thorpe Park next month, where the entire ride has been custom-built with VR at its heart. (And crucially built indoors, where it'll be much easier to manipulate the environment to fit the story.)

Why VR Improves Roller Coasters - and Roller Coasters Improve VR

First published March 30, 2016

One week after riding The New Revolution at Six Flags Magic Mountain, I'm still thinking about how much I enjoyed my first ride on a virtual reality roller coaster.

As I mentioned in my review of The New Revolution, I was skeptical about whether VR on a coaster would be too extreme. Like many other doubters, I wondered if I'd come off the coaster ready to lose my lunch. But as I rode The New Revolution, I discovered that the addition of virtual reality actually helped make this one of the most comfortable rides I'd ever experienced on a roller coaster.

How could that be? That question has been nagging me for several days, so I'd like to share some of what I've been thinking over that time. First, though, it's important to clarify a few concepts, so that we can start this conversation in the same place. These concepts get conflated in some people's minds, but they're really three distinct ideas that ought to be considered as such. They are: Virtual Reality, Augmented Reality, and Computer Generated Imagery.

Virtual Reality completely obstructs your view of the "real" world with whatever video is shown on the VR screen that is strapped across your eyes. Augmented reality does not block your entire view of whatever is around you, but uses clear or partial screens to impose video imagery into whatever you see "in real life." Computer Generated Imagery [CGI] is what VR and AR typically uses to create whatever video you see on those screens. CGI has become ubiquitous in movies, displacing the models, animatronics, and matte painting that moviemakers used to employ to create special effects.

The New Revolution, like all of Six Flags' new coasters, uses Virtual Reality, meaning that you won't see any of the views fans are used to seeing on these coasters — unless you decide not to wear the provided VR headset, of course. No one has developed an Augmented Reality coaster yet, but that's the next step I cannot wait to experience. AR promises the potential of the best of both worlds — the heights and other practical visuals from riding a roller coaster, coupled with CGI storytelling.

But let's get back to the skepticism. I think a large part of that grew from movie fans' frustration with how filmmakers have abused CGI over the years. Take a moment to read this great post, 6 Reasons Modern Movie CGI Looks Surprisingly Crappy [http://www.cracked.com/blog/6-reasons-expensive-films-end-up-with-crappy-special-effects/], paying special attention to "Lack Of Visual Restraint Makes Gravity Act Like A Cartoon" and "Most Films Forget That A Camera Needs To Physically Exist."

Since almost all VR relies on CGI, the sins of the one are often attributed to the other. It's bad enough to sit in stationary theater and watch CGI from directors who ignore the laws of physics. No one wants to do that while riding a moving roller coaster at the same time.

But putting VR on a roller coaster forces creators to obey those laws of physics that they can get away with ignoring in movies. If you are going to synchronize the action on the VR screen with the movement of a roller coaster, you can't start moving and gyrating in unnatural ways. You have to go with the flow of the physical coaster. And that enforces a more natural sequence of motion in the VR, one that removes much of the discomfort that moviegoers feel with poorly-storyboarded CGI.

With the motion on screen in sync with motion of the ride, we also can avoid the physical disconnect that viewers typically feel when they see wildly gyrating POV on the screen while sitting in stationary seats. I think many fans feared that they would be seeing that same, physics-defying CGI in their VR headsets, while riding a coaster whose movements wouldn't — and couldn't — match the crazy action on screen.

That is why so many fans have feared VR coasters, IMHO. But in reality, roller coasters improve VR by forcing directors to behave themselves.

And VR can help improve roller coasters by injecting some fresh excitement into aging mid-range rides whose specs too often leave them in the "no fans land" between family coasters and the latest world-class thrill rides. Smart use of VR can leave fans wanting to ride again and again on coasters that otherwise might quickly lose their appeal. Heck, on a VR coaster, maybe some squeamish riders might even be able to overcome their fear of heights and agree to ride. After all, they'll never see where they are above the ground.

If VR allows parks to justify rebuilding tracks, installing new trains, and otherwise refurbishing coasters to provide the smoother ride that best complements a VR installation, that's great news even for fans who decline to ride with the headsets, too.

So instead of VR and coasters creating the most unholy mash-up since Batman fought Superman (sorry — no, not sorry), VR coasters give fans that business-school cliche — a "win-win."

With The New Revolution, Six Flags has given skeptics reason to believe that VR and coasters can be a great mix. (Some might still doubt whether VR headsets and safety straps can be kept clean over an entire summer, but that's another post.) And as much as I enjoyed The New Revolution, Theme Park Insider Ben Mills reports that Alton Towers' Galactica might be even better (see comments above).

If enough fans give VR coasters a try, maybe companies will hire more designers and developers to advance VR storytelling in theme parks, creating new adventures for fans to enjoy. That's a trend that even the most skeptical fans ought to be willing to embrace.

Readers respond:

Flavio de Souza: What if... people are allowed to bring their own headset? On the night before going to your local Six Flags or Cedar Fair theme park you enter in the App Store, look to the coasters you will be riding in the next day, and, for each coaster, you could have three or four different options of themes to choose.

You could choose a fighter theme, a Superman, a Marvel (no east/west of Mississippi rules would apply here), or even a Star Wars. You would download and pay for it.

The theme park would offer only the physical platform, and would not need to worry with development costs or pay for character licensing. This could be a real game changer!

Sarah Warner: @Flavio, a remarkable idea! But I cannot imagine that the Samsung phones used in these Gear VR headsets would be typical "off the shelf" units. One can only assume there is hardware also on the coaster side that signals and interacts with the headsets to insure they are indeed synched. It probably also updates the headsets along the track to indicate where in the "action" it should be. Coasters move at different speeds based on their weight load so the headsets need to know that as well. But I agree, I'd rather wear my own VR headset than share one.

Robert Niles: Sarah brings up good points. The sync is everything. But looking far into the future, when VR and AR might become as ubiquitous as smartphones are now, perhaps parks might simply offer an app that fans can download to sync their personal VR/AR unit with the coaster they want to ride.

As for the question about feel, I didn't notice any weight from the headset on the ride. With the straps tightened properly, the headset is very comfortable.

Simonjohn74: I rode Galactica on Tuesday at Alton Towers. There is no age restriction for wearing the headsets on Galactica. My daughter, who is eight, rode with me, and she chose to wear the headset and is now a VR coaster convert like me. The experience is very difficult to describe, but if the VR is done well, like it is on Galactica, it is a seamless ride experience that easily makes you feel like you are flying through space. You easily can forget you are just riding a coaster with a screen attached to your head. The headsets themselves are extremely comfortable and not in anyway heavy or bulky.

However, unlike Six Flags, Galactica do not change the headset between riders as they are fastened to the restraints. They are, however, cleaned with a wipe between riders. I'm not sure how often the headsets are changed and completely cleaned, but that could be an issue especially for germophobes as by the end of the day the headset will have been on a lot of different possibly sweaty or greasy heads. If you can cope with this, it is an experience I would completely recommend you try.

I had my reservations before I rode but I would now not go back to riding Galactica without the headset. On a slightly separate note, people keep mentioning the theming of the coaster, apart from the loading bay you do not see any other part of the coaster whilst on the ride so theming from a riders point of view is not important, Galactica have installed a smoking space portal at the bottom of the first drop but when you are on the ride you have no idea when you pass through it, it is just for the benefit of visitors watching the ride from the ground.

AJ Hummel: After trying New Revolution yesterday, I have to say that VR is a great idea on coasters when used properly. If you've got an older coaster that isn't pulling the crowds anymore, offering VR on the ride is likely to increase ridership. However, VR does somewhat defeat the purpose of a roller coaster being a roller coaster, instead converting it into a weird experience that lies somewhere between a coaster and a motion simulator. It should never be mandatory for any ride, and it is not something I would want to do every time. It is also not something that should be applied to every ride…one VR coaster per park would be fine with me, but it will become too gimmicky if every ride has it (just like Universal and 3D simulators).

Stephen Tuday: Having tried the VR coaster at Six Flags over Georgia (Dare Devil Dive), I have to say it was amazing. The technology behind this will only get better as time goes on and the possibilities seem limitless. Comparing a VR coaster to a traditional ride (without VR) is comparing apples to oranges. They are two different experiences and I will still enjoy riding non-VR coasters as well. The argument was once "wooden vs. steel"; now it will be "VR vs. traditional!"

Nonetheless, this is all very exciting. My only fear is that the VR technology will give parks an excuse NOT to add new thrill rides. I mean... why invest millions in a new coaster when you can take an older coaster and give it a VR makeover for a tiny fraction of the cost? (I hope I am not giving any theme park big wigs any ideas...)

Ultimately it will be coaster fans that drive the development of VR. The more folks that give it a try will translate to more research and development and thus even more amazing experiences in the near future. I can't wait!

What's the Next Big Thing in Theme Park Ride Technology?
First published October 7, 2016

New technology gives theme parks new ways to tell their stories. From tubular steel roller coasters allowing Arrow and Disney to send riders sliding down the Matterhorn, to flight simulators allowing Disney to send people on tours of the Star Wars universe, to factory robot arms allowing Universal to make enchanted benches fly through the wizarding world, theme parks have found wonderful new ways to entertain fans by embracing new ride tech.

So what's the next new development that will revolutionize theme park attractions? Based upon what we've seen in the past couple of years, you might think it's virtual reality. Six Flags has been adding VR to roller coasters at many of its theme parks, while Universal and other companies have been adding upcharge VR experiences to their Halloween events.

In my Orange County Register column this week, I suggest that VR might not be the next big thing in the industry... but it might represent a step toward that next big thing, instead. Here's the big problem with VR: Virtual reality robs theme parks of their greatest strength in the entertainment business — the creation of intricately decorated, immersively themed physical spaces that can't be experienced anywhere else. When all visitors see is a VR screen, theme parks lose the value of the physical environments they've spent so much money to create.

But what if parks could put together the best of both worlds... and show VR animation in a way that allowed people to keep seeing all that wonderfully themed physical space in the park around them? That's augmented reality, and that might be the next big thing in theme parks.

To employ AR in theme parks, though, tech developers and creative designers need to learn some lessons from VR and the way guests react to it. More than anything else, we would need AR headsets that are just as inexpensive and even easier to use than today's VR headsets. If parks and tech companies could develop augmented reality glasses that are as easy to make, distribute, and use as today's 3D glasses, then parks could unlock a new dimension in themed storytelling.

Imagine Universal's planned Nintendo lands with the power of augmented reality. That would provide an experience that would be true to the look, feel and functionality of Nintendo's video games, within a practical environment that no screen ever could recreate. The blend of the virtual and the practical would give theme parks an advantage over any in-home VR entertainment alternative, and the scope of practical detail in a theme park would make it the preferred venue for any AR experience.

But to get to AR on a large scale in theme parks, we must endure some of the frustrations of learning about mass implementations of VR first. That's why I don't get too upset about slow load times for VR roller coasters or the added cost of a VR monster maze. Theme parks and the technology partners are learning from these experiences, and what they could be able to develop after learning those lessons might turn out to be the most amazing things we've seen in theme parks yet.

Readers react:

AJ Hummel: I think you're right about VR being a limited time thing and AR becoming the next successful innovation. In fact, I'd be shocked if it isn't used in some way in Universal's Nintendo Land. The problem is always going to be that it needs to be convincing to be worthwhile, and that is one of the problems that virtual attractions tend to have. As good as Transformers may be, I've never thought it felt real, while something like Pirates of the Caribbean does give that feeling. If a virtual attraction can be both something that can't be experienced elsewhere and something that feels real, it could be the greatest attraction ever built. Otherwise, it will likely be very popular, but ultimately become dated and cheesy. There's a reason many Disney attractions can often last 40-50 years but some Universal attractions struggle to survive two decades, and it isn't just the IP.

Tony Perkins: When they create a holodeck, then I'll be interested.

A WIZARD MOVES WEST: UNIVERSAL BRINGS HARRY POTTER TO HOLLYWOOD

Five years after announcing it, Universal Studios Hollywood opened its Wizarding World of Harry Potter land this year. The centerpiece of the park's ongoing billion-dollar-plus transformation, Universal's fourth Harry Potter-themed land worldwide was expected to boost attendance at a park that's been enjoying a hot streak in recent years, despite the disruption of all that construction work.

If you've visited the original Wizarding World of Harry Potter at Universal Orlando's Islands of Adventure park, you might notice a few differences between that version of Hogsmeade village and the Wizarding World Hollywood. The biggest is the absence of the Dragon Challenge B&M Inverted coasters in Hollywood. But Hollywood's Wizarding World offers the 3D version of Harry Potter and the Forbidden Journey, which debuted in 2014 at Universal Studios Japan. Other differences include:

Ollivander's is located on the other side of High Street, and includes a second theater and expanded wand shop.

Gladrags Wizardwear takes Ollivanders' place next to Owl Post.

There are two additional interactive wand windows in

Hollywood's Wizarding World.

The Weasley's Ford Anglia is found in an expanded outdoor queue for Forbidden Journey, as there is no Dragon Challenge queue for it here.

Flight of the Hippogriff is a Mack Youngster coaster instead of a Vekoma Junior, though the ride is quite similar.

Zonko's is back, although in abbreviated form. It closed in Orlando for an expansion of Honeydukes.

The restrooms use the same themed design as those in Diagon Alley in Orlando.

The Three Broomsticks offers an expanded menu, including many items from Orlando's Leaky Cauldron, plus a "Sunday Roast" prime rib main course.

There's no Hot Butterbeer or Butterbeer Ice Cream at The Three Broomsticks. (At least not yet.)

The lockers next to the Hogwarts Express photo op have been replaced with a pay photo op of the interior of a Hogwarts Express compartment.

Appropriate to the Scottish Highlands setting, Hollywood's Wizarding World is the first to include actual mountains in the distance, surrounding the land.

For your reference, here is the complete line-up of everything in Universal Studios Hollywood's Wizarding World of Harry Potter.

Attractions:

- Harry Potter and the Forbidden Journey (3D version)
- Flight of the Hippogriff
- Ollivander's

Shows:

- Frog Choir

- Triwizard Spirit Rally

Food and Beverages:

- The Three Broomsticks
- Hog's Head Pub
- Two Butterbeer carts (One at each entrance to the land)

Shops:

- Zonko's Joke Shop
- Honeydukes
- Dervish and Banges
- Owl Post
- Gladrags Wizardwear
- Wiseacre's Wizarding Equipment
- Filch's Emporium of Confiscated Goods (Located the exit of Harry Potter and the Forbidden Journey)

Wizarding World of Harry Potter Soft-Opens at Universal Studios Hollywood
First published February 12, 2016

Shortly before 3 this afternoon, the Wizarding World of Harry Potter soft-opened to visitors for the first time at Universal Studios Hollywood.

A crowds of about 300 visitors had gathered in a holding area, some waiting there since the park had opened at 9am. Those waiting were given the first entry passes into the new land, with other park guests admitted after that. Which resulted in wait time throughout the park evaporating as thousands of fans rushed into Hogsmeade.

This wasn't a half-hearted soft open, either. All locations in the Wizarding World were open and functional, including Harry Potter and the Forbidden Journey, the Flying Hippogriff, the Three Broomsticks, the Hog's Head Pub, Ollivander's, and all the stores. Even the "magic" windows were operational, allowing visitors to case spells with Universal's interactive wands. (I brought the one I got in Orlando.)

Having spent much of the day waiting, I started my visit in The Three Broomsticks. The bangers and mash ($12.99) were even better than the ones in the Leaky Cauldron at Universal Orlando's Diagon Alley. And I'll give a big thumbs-up to the Butterbeer Potter Cream dessert ($5.29). And, of course, there's Butterbeer. My precioussssss....

After The Three Broomsticks, I warmed up for Forbidden Journey with a trip on Universal Studios Hollywood's first outdoor roller coaster, The Flying Hippogriff. But the land's signature attraction, of course, is Harry Potter and the Forbidden Journey, which is presented here in 3D. Of course, there are a few changes in the queue, too, including the Weasleys' Ford Anglia being here in an extended outdoor queue, as there is no Dragon Challenge roller coaster here in California.

Once inside Hogwarts Castle, I opted to skip the hour-long wait by using the convenient single-rider lane, which took me straight to the Gryffindor common room, then into the Room of Requirement. The 3D glasses here were the standard model found on rides such as Transformers, and not the custom Quidditch goggles found at Universal Studios Japan. I found the glasses a hassle on the ride, as they kept sliding off my nose as my flying bench swirled through the attraction. Perhaps Universal will get the better-fitting goggle-style glasses in stock by the land's official opening on April 7. [Editor's addition: They did.]

The 3D version of the film didn't do anything for me over the traditional version at Universal Orlando. It seemed a bit oversaturated at times, and the 3D didn't really "pop" - still seeming two dimensional in comparison with the abundant practical sets and effects in the ride.

If you are visiting Universal Studios Hollywood this weekend, use the hashtag #PotterWatch on social media to ket other visitors know when the Wizarding World is open. As will all "technical rehearsals," openings are not guaranteed, and attractions might open or close at any time.

Vague Thoughts on a Soft Opening: The Wizarding World Hollywood
First published February 20, 2016, by Douglas Hindley

Disclaimer: The world does not need another review of the Wizarding World of Harry Potter. It certainly doesn't need one inspired by a single day of soft openings. It certainly, certainly doesn't need such a review from a theme park fan so profoundly ignorant, he can only claim five parks to his name, all in Southern California. (Okay, technically I've been to Tokyo Disneyland also, but they weren't open yet. They let me wear an adorable baby-sized hard hat and everything! True story.) Nonetheless, if you'll allow it, here are the nonsensical ramblings of a fellow who made it out to Universal Studios Hollywood this past Sunday on a total Valentine's Day whim, to check out the "new" Harry Potter land.

Altogether, WWOHP is a fantastic land, and an even better, a fantastic addition to USH. Due to its size and available land space, the Hollywood park has always lagged Florida. It gets by on the tram tour, but it's never really had anything like themed lands. Remember, USH is ground zero for the "studio park," where barebones soundstages house whatever IP was randomly deemed most profitable at the time of installation. Much of USH's "place-making" has been with post-modern silliness – the studio park trick of admitting to their own fakeness. This helped set USH apart from Disney at the time.

But they've been edging ever closer to being a true theme park lately. With Harry Potter, USH can boast a whopping nine rides (six or seven of those E-tickets), where once they just had the tram tour and some supporting shows. With tiny acreage, attractions alone can only do so much. The brilliance of WWOHP in USH is that the land itself extends the time a guest spends on its acreage, much more than "Forbidden Journey" could do on its own. It's a very different way to tour USH than one does on the Lower Lot, where you just run between the three (awesome) rides, then wander off. And the guests I saw used WWOHP as it was intended: grown men in wizard costumes, children testing wands on every storefront, nearly every guest fully engaging with each minor nicety.

By USH standards, this WWOHP is immersive. You can still see some outside distractions, most beyond Universal's control. Nearby skyscrapers loom over the quaint cottages. Heck, I glimpsed the Warner Bros. backlot from within Hogwarts! Plus the distant mountains covered in suburban sprawl. These are all unavoidable facts of USH's location.

Immersion breaking moments which Universal could control – Springfield is visible from the "Forbidden Journey" entrance. (Springfield is USH's former most immersive spot, a complete "Simpsons" land, but it's too garish and cartoony vs. Potter's semi-realism to work as well in a theme park environment.) From the Three Broomsticks and other spots I could see the "Forbidden Journey" show-building beside its façade. And there are prominent speaker poles and misters erected in queues, useful, yet odd for a land which wants no detail out of place.

But WWOHP's batting average is great! People talk about how in Florida it created a new degree of immersion never before seen in any theme park ever, ever, ever. Every product, every cast member interaction, all work towards immersion. There's no Coke, only Pumpkin Juice. I'm surprised they accept U.S. currency. In truth, Universal just fine-tuned and rediscovered something which has been around at least as long as Main Street U.S.A. or Knott's Ghost Town. In 1955, Disneyland;s Main Street was a lot closer to a genuine small town, with a barber shop and bra store and such. New Orleans Square was similar. Disney's error has been to oversaturate every section of their parks with the same generic

Disney style, until Main Street became just a really nice looking mall. (Eisner's self-conscious attempts to undermine theme for profits — this is what Disney stood for when Potter first premiered.) But Disney is moving away from that, slowly.

I think the reason people would call Potter more effective than these old-school lands is due to Potter's one-franchise focus. This is a near-literal duplication of locations seen in some films and books, so it's really, really easy to connect with audiences. Who today could connect to a 1900 small town as easily? It takes more imagination and more effort (on the guest's part) to engage with a non-branded, semi-historical location. But as Potter fades with time, as "Cars" fades, will their lands still work? I think so, at least with these examples. If the settings appeal regardless of IP, they'll last. I sort of detest the "Cars" films, yet I adore Cars Land's retro desert vibe. I'm indifferent towards Potter, but the idea of a wizard's village could have worked even without an IP. I think WWOHP leans a little heavy on the guest's familiarity with the source material. But it works.

"Forbidden Journey" is a fantastic experience, queue and all! The queue is Indy-level brilliant. The locker setup, though, is a bonkers free-for-all. My only complaint with the ride is, curiously, the addition: the 3D. The spex blocked my field of vision, and they darkened the non-screen parts of the ride. My second time through, I took the glasses off for the dark ride sections, and my experience improved immensely. (Reportedly, these soft opening glasses were stolen from "Transformers" using a Cloak of Invisibility, so some upcoming spectacles might improve the spectacle.) I also suspect that the ride's intensity has been toned down in order to keep the glasses from magically vanishing. Perhaps this is Universal's sneaky attempt to lower the height limit and make a (slightly) more family-friendly ride.

"Flight of the Hippogriff" – the family coaster – is bipolar. Where it is themed, it is beautiful. Hagrid's cottage, the wicker ride baskets, the bric-a-brac in the loading station. And yet… it's a bare-naked roller coaster. The track is painted the same tones as the local landscaping, but still. I'm fine with a coaster, in the proper setting, but when Potter does so much to appear accurate, this stands out. I understand they needed more than one ride, and in IOA this was grandfathered in from the pre-Potter land, but it is new construction here. It's a minor intrusion, but it grates.

Food and snacks and such were all fine. Butterbeer is neat, though it's no vodka. The pub grub was slightly below the quality served at my local watering hole, which means for a theme park it was exceptional. I loved exploring the shop interiors, admiring every item for sale, and every moving, animated detail in the nooks and crannies. That right there, those animated details, those are the best thing about WWOHP. I looked up from a Butterbeer queue once and saw a magical imp dash into a chimney. (This wasn't my first Butterbeer, so I might've just been hallucinating.) Some say they could visit WWOHP, do no rides, and still be satisfied. This is true.

These kinetic movements, lived-in details, sensible products, in-character employees – the best of what a theme park can do. WWOHP combines these qualities more consistently than you'll usually find. Potter is the perfect vehicle for this, a world which was already fully-realized and pleasant.

I had fun!

We Ate All the Main Courses at The Three Broomsticks

First published March 14, 2016 (Prices below were as of the original publication date.)

We needed several visits to complete the task, but in the interest of serving you, our Theme Park Insider readers, we ordered and ate every main course at Universal Studios Hollywood's The Three Broomsticks. A sacrifice, we know.

There are nowhere near any bad selections among the eight main courses offered at the restaurant in Universal's Wizarding World of Harry Potter, which is now open for "technical rehearsals" in advance of the land's April 7 official opening. But we will help you choose what to order on your first go around this enticing menu with our notes below. Keep in mind: We paid for it all — no special media invitation or accommodations for this one.

(Pro tip: Wait a minute or two after you get your Butterbeer for the butterscotch foam to bubble up to peak volume before drinking it, to get the full experience of its flavor.)

If you have visited either of the Wizarding World land in Orlando, we would recommend ordering the one dish that is unique to the Wizarding World Hollywood: The Sunday Roast ($21.99). The roast beef is served to order and comes with vegetables, sliced roasted potatoes, a Yorkshire pudding, and au jus. It's just a stunning meal for a theme park counter-service restaurant and well worth ordering any day of the week.

The Three Broomsticks is supposed to be a Scottish pub, so you might wish to opt for the meals traditionally found on pub menus. My favorite among those is the Bangers & Mash ($12.99). The highlight of this dish is the deeply-flavored onion gravy that distinguishes a great bangers & mash beyond a simple plate of sausages and potatoes. This selection comes with minty English peas and a roasted tomato — two more delightfully British accents to the meal.

My love for the Bangers & Mash is not to take away from the equally tasty Beef, Lamb & Guinness Stew ($13.99), though. Rich with chunks of beef, lamb, and root vegetables in a Guinness-infused sauce, this stew just demolishes any other bread bowl meal we've had before in a theme park. It's enough to make you wish for colder weather in LA, to more properly enjoy the warmth of this dish.

You can't go wrong with The Three Broomsticks' Fish & Chips ($14.99), either. With an airy, crispy batter providing a nice contrast with the rich, flaky fish, this meal also includes wedge-cut fries. The tartar sauce is a touch on the sweet side, but there's so much flavor in the fish that we usually just skip it in favor of a squeeze of the provided lemon, anyway.

The Shepherd's Pie ($12.99) is pure comfort food. (And yes, as it includes ground beef, it properly should be called a cottage pie instead of a shepherd's pie, which includes ground lamb. But we're not Gordon Ramsay, so screw it. For what it's worth, Universal does call this dish a Cottage Pie at the Leaky Cauldron in Orlando.) Of the traditional pub meals on the Three Broomsticks' menu, this dish ranks below the meals above for me... mostly because as an American living in Los Angeles — where it's perpetually 70 degrees and sunny — Shepherd's Pie just doesn't push the emotional buttons that it would for someone who grew up enjoying this simple casserole of ground beef, vegetables, and mashed potatoes on cold, overcast days. But the accompanying mixed greens salad is amazing for a theme park side dish — we recommend highly the Stilton blue cheese dressing.

Now we get to three dishes that might not be authentic, but certainly hold their own on this menu.

The Spare Ribs ($16.99) might be among the best we've ever had — meaty without fat or gristle and with a tangy sauce that doesn't overwhelm the rich pork flavor of the ribs.

The half dozen ribs are served with corn on the cob and roasted sliced potatoes, as are the chicken and turkey leg entrees. That Lemon Herb Roasted Chicken ($13.99) is just as good as the ribs, with an accompanying garlic herb sauce for the half chicken that would drive Count Dracula out of his home studio, if he ever were allowed to get near it. If you are interested, and visiting with family or friends, you can order the ribs and chicken together, along with a family-sized salad, in The Three Broomsticks' The Great Feast ($54.99), which serves four.

Back to the individual main courses, that leave us with the Turkey Leg ($13.99). That the rest of the dishes at The Three Broomsticks can make a smoked turkey leg seem "meh" in comparison probably ought to tell you all you need to know about the quality and variety of this restaurant.

While we were eating all these main courses, of course we had to order all the desserts, as well, including Butterbeer Potted Cream ($5.29) and a Sticky Toffee Pudding ($6.99). The toffee pudding was my favorite of The Three Broomsticks' desserts, with its chocolate surprise lurking within. (Pro tip #2: Don't drink a Butterbeer with the Toffee Pudding. The stronger taste of the Toffee Pudding will reduce the Butterbeer to tasting like a foamy Seltzer.)

The Apple Pie ($3.89) was a close second for me, with abundant juicy apple slices within a warm cinnamon-laden crust. It pairs wonderfully with the Pumpkin Juice ($4.39), which tastes like you are drinking a pumpkin pie.

That Butterbeer Potted Cream tastes just like the liquid Butterbeer, too, making it a bit redundant if you're drinking one with your meal. But if you opt for the Pumpkin Juice, or one of The Three Broomsticks' adult beverages (draught beers are $10.99), wrapping up with a Butterbeer Potted Cream is a perfect way to get a taste of that flavor in your meal, instead.

Finally, we have the Chocolate Trifle ($4.39). If you believe, as my daughter says, that "it's not really dessert if it doesn't have chocolate," this is the selection for you. Topped with shaved chocolate and a cocoa ladyfinger above a layer of raspberry sauce and a base of chocolate mousse, this trifle should satisfy any chocolate lover.

In addition these main courses and desserts, The Three Broomsticks serves a Roast Chicken salad ($9.89) and a Soup & Salad Combo ($9.49, with a choice of Corn, English Ale & Cheddar, or Leek & Potato soups). Children's meals are $7.29 each and the options are Fish & Chips, a Chicken Quarter, Chicken Tenders, and Macaroni Cheese. Ice cream is available for $4.99 and comes in vanilla, chocolate, and strawberry and peanut butter flavors. As of now, there's no Butterbeer ice cream (or hot Butterbeer) available at the Wizarding World in Hollywood.

But what here is more than enough to move Universal Studios Hollywood's The Three Broomsticks into strong contention among the world's best theme park counter service restaurants. And along with last year's addition of the restaurants in the adjacent Springfield USA, Universal Studios Hollywood is now the place to eat for hungry theme park fans in Southern California.

The Wizarding World Hollywood Opens Officially
First published April 7, 2016

Universal Studios Hollywood this morning officially opened its Wizarding World of Harry Potter to thousands of enthusiastic Potter fans.

Park president Larry Kurzweil brought Harry Potter film stars Warwick Davis, Tom Felton, Evanna Lynch, James Phelps, and Oliver Phelps to the Hogsmeade gate to help open the land, which was revealed after hundreds of fans at the gate cast a "Revelio" charm.

Some fans camped overnight at the park to be among the first in line to experience the centerpiece of Universal Studios Hollywood's billion-dollar expansion plan. Universal Studios Hollywood's Wizarding World follows two successful Harry Potter-themed lands at the Universal Orlando Resort, and one at Universal Studios Japan, which has propelled Universal's most popular theme park to record attendance.

About two thousand fans appeared to be in the park for the land's 6:30am opening, far fewer than tens of thousands who crammed Universal's Islands of Adventure theme park for the opening of the original Wizarding World in June 2010. But Universal opened the Hollywood version at the crack of dawn on a Thursday during the school year, instead of at the height of the summer season. Nevertheless, the park announced that it had sold out all available advance-sale tickets for the day. Universal recently introduced a new ticketing system that ties advance sale tickets to a specific date of use, with varying discounts based upon the planned date of visit, in part to better distribute the large crowds that the Wizarding World is expected to attract to the park, which has posted strong attendance gains in recent years anyway.

Universal swiftly activated its timed-ticket system for Wizarding World entry this morning. When I left, shortly before 8am, visitors were getting return times about two hours after requesting a ticket. And once inside the land, the wait for Forbidden Journey was three hours.

The Wizarding World in Hollywood began "technical rehearsals" in February, allowing thousands of fans the opportunity to experience the land in advance of the official opening.

[Late update] By 4pm, afternoon rain had cleared the park somewhat. Return time tickets were available for pretty much an immediate return, and the FJ wait was down to about 30 minutes. Clearly, Southern Californians love British magical villages… but not in anything like British weather.

DUBAI ENTERS THE THEME PARK BUSINESS

When the global economy tanked in 2008, it dragged many new theme park deals down with it. Several of those developments were scheduled for Dubai and the United Arab Emirates. Plans for Universal, SeaWorld, Busch Gardens, and Six Flags theme parks in the area were abandoned, and "Dubai" became a metaphor in the theme park fan community for unrealistic plans.

But as the economy revived, so did plans for theme parks in Dubai. The emirate's leadership remained committed to tourism as the focus of a post-oil economy in the area, and in 2016 theme park developments began to move from proposal to reality. The world's largest indoor theme park, IMG Worlds of Adventure, opened in August, the big development was Dubai Parks and Resorts.

Featuring three theme parks, a water park, a hotel and a shopping and dining district, Dubai Parks & Resorts is the perhaps the most ambitious theme park development in the industry's history. No other resort has attempted to open multiple parks at essentially the same time. Originally scheduled for an October 31 debut, only Legoland Dubai hit that target, with Bollywood Parks pushed back into November and the movie-themed Motiongate Dubai scheduled for a December opening.

Let's Look at the Attraction Line-up for Motiongate Dubai
First published April 12, 2016

With new virtual reality roller coasters and a new Harry Potter land, 2016 already has seen some exciting new additions to major theme parks around the world. And the rush of new attractions will continue in the weeks ahead, with the opening of Ninjago: The Ride at Legoland California next month, Skull Island: Reign of Kong at Universal Orlando's Islands of Adventure in June, and new Frozen attractions at Walt Disney World and Disneyland later this spring and summer.

But we've got some entire new parks debuting in 2016, as well. You probably already know about Shanghai Disneyland, so let's take a few moments to introduce you to Motiongate Dubai.

Opening in October [Update: Yeah, that didn't happen....], Motiongate Dubai will be a movie-themed park with franchises from DreamWorks Animation, Lionsgate, and Sony, including The Hunger Games, Underworld, Ghostbusters, Zombieland, The Green Hornet, Hotel Transylvania, Cloudy with a Chance of Meatballs, The Smurfs, Shrek, Madagascar, Kung Fu Panda, and How to Train Your Dragon.

The park is the flagship of the new US$2.9 billion Dubai Parks and Resorts in Jebel Ali. Given the often, uh, challenging heat in the United Arab Emirates, the majority of Motiongate Dubai's attractions will be located indoors, opening some interesting creative theming opportunities for the park's designers.

The park will be divided into five themed lands, with three of the five devoted to the three participating movie studios. Let's take a look at the attraction line-up, starting at the entrance and moving counter-clockwise:

Studio Central

- Park entrance plaza, with dining and shopping

Sony Pictures Studios

- Hotel Transylvania (Dark ride)
- Cloudy with a Chance of Meatballs: River Expedition (Rapids ride)
- Flint's Imagination Lab (Playground)
- Zombieland: Blast Off (Drop ride)
- Ghostbusters: Battle for New York (Shooter ride)
- The Green Hornet: High Speed Chase (Roller coaster)
- Underworld 4D (4D show)

Smurfs Village

- Smurfs Studio Tour (Family ride)
- Smurfs Village Playhouse (Theater show)
- Smurfs Village Express (Family coaster)
- Woodland Play Park (Playground)
- Smurfberry Factory (Kiddie playground)

DreamWorks Animation

- Shrek's Merry Fairy Tale Journey (Dark ride)
- Swamp Celebration (Spinner)
- Madagascar Mad Pursuit (Roller coaster)
- Melman Go-Round (Carousel)
- Penguin Air (Swing ride)
- Kung Fu Panda: Unstoppable Awesomeness (4D show)
- Mr. Ping's Noodle Fling (Teacups)

- Kung Fu Panda Academy (Theater show)
- Dragon Gliders (Suspended coaster)
- Camp Viking (Water playground)
- Swinging Viking (Swinging ship)

Lionsgate

- Capitol Bullet Train (Roller coaster)
- Panem Aerial Tour (Motion simulator)
- Step Up Dubai, All In! (Musical show)

The park will offer nine themed restaurants across the five lands, as well.

In addition to Motiongate Dubai, the Dubai Parks and Resorts complex will include two other theme parks: Legoland Dubai and Bollywood Dubai. We'll be writing more about Motiongate Dubai in the weeks leading up to its opening.

Readers respond:

James Trexen: Sounds like a pretty well-rounded park and I'm especially glad to see Ghostbusters and Zombieland still getting the love. Whether or not the Hunger Games is viable for a theme park remains to be seen, but I'm looking forward to some on-ride videos.

From an anonymous reader: Of all the IPs being used for this park, the one that makes me scratch my head more than anything else is Green Hornet.

While Underworld and Zombieland haven't really been talked about that much in recent years, they were still popular at one point, so it's kinda understandable. But I don't think Green Hornet was ever popular. I don't think it was that much of a hit at the box office and I don't think the people who actually saw it really liked it that much. So, yeah, I don't really see how they expect this movie to draw in any big crowds.

Robert Niles: Some interesting points about Dubai: Most of its visitors come from the Middle East, Europe, and South Asia, in that order. The next most popular markets sending tourists to Dubai are Southeast Asia, the Far East, and Russia... followed by all of the Americas. Subsaharan Africa is the only region that sends fewer visitors to Dubai that North and South America, combined.

So... it's not our thing in America. We're not the target market and Dubai can do very well without us. However, it's a HUGE and growing destination for Europeans. (How many football kits have I seen advertising airlines and other businesses in the UAE?) And it's a HUGE market for themed entertainment designers in the U.S. Heck, two of the firms working on this are located within three miles of my home in Southern California.

Yeowser: Is it just me or the attraction lineup for Motiongate Dubai sounds better than the starting lineup for Shanghai Disneyland? As for the Green Hornet attraction, one of the better attractions at Disney World is Dinosaur at Animal Kingdom, based on a movie not many people remember, including me.

Dubai Parks Releases its Theme Song, from Disney's Alan Menken
First published August 7, 2016

Dubai Parks and Resorts today released its official theme song for the resort, which opens in October. Written by Alan Menken — a name that will be very familiar to Disney fans — the song, "All the Wonders of the Universe," features in an original eight-minute animated film that also creates a fanciful origin story for the multi-park resort.

Composer Menken is an eight-time Academy Award winner (and official "Disney Legend") who got his start with the late Howard Ashman on "Little Shop of Horrors," before scoring a string of Disney hits, including The Little Mermaid, Beauty and the

Beast, and Newsies. His "Compass of your Heart" probably would be one of the most popular songs ever written exclusively for a theme park if it were in a ride at Walt Disney World instead of at Tokyo DisneySea, where relatively few theme park fans outside of Japan ever get to visit.

In a press release, Menken said, "Writing the song and score for the Dubai Parks and Resorts project was fun and unique for me in many ways. Creating a central theme to inaugurate the park called upon the experience I've gained working with the Disney company; to encapsulate the concept of this particular park in a larger-than-life song and message. For inspiration I drew on the story that the Dubai Parks and Resorts team presented to me and imagined how a magical them park might spring to life in the middle of the desert. I really believe that the song 'All the Wonders of the Universe' is a perfect fit for this amazing new destination."

Dubai Parks and Resorts will open three parks this fall: Motiongate, Bollywood Parks, and Legoland Dubai. We've written several posts about Motiongate Dubai, which will be a movie-themed resorts featuring franchises from DreamWorks Animation, Sony Pictures Studios and Lionsgate. The Legoland will be the first in the Middle East, and the Bollywood park will feature India's popular musical film industry. A second phase will follow in 2019, and is slated to include the Middle East's first Six Flags theme park.

Here's Your First Look at Six Flags Dubai
First published May 3, 2016

Six Flags this morning released its first detailed concept art for its planned theme park in Dubai. Six Flags Dubai is scheduled to open in late 2019 as the part of phase two of the Dubai Parks and Resorts development, which will open this October with Motiongate Dubai, Legoland Dubai, and Bollywood Park Dubai.

The Six Flags park will be the first thrill park in the Persian Gulf region and will feature 27 attractions, according to Six Flags' press release. Design firm FORREC is creating the park, in conjunction with Six Flags.

Given the typical heat in the United Arab Emirates, the park will feature an indoor, air-conditioned entry plaza, though most of the attractions will be located outdoors. From Six Flags' press release:

Guests will enter and exit the park through an impressive, state-of-the-art promenade. The fully air-conditioned area will offer a VIP mezzanine, space for private and catered events, along with an assortment of retail and food locations including a signature bakery and deli. Guests will have access to three attractions from inside the plaza and the park's signature roller coaster will encircle the entire promenade.

Early concept art typically provides more of an impression of what a park will look like, rather than a faithful representation of its ultimate form. But there's enough detail in the concept art that we can start taking educated guesses what some of those 27 attractions will be.

We know from the press release that one attraction will be "a next generation 4-D interactive dark ride," so let's assume that the big show building in Six Flags' concept art will be Justice League: Battle for Metropolis. Beyond that, moving counterclockwise around the park, we see:

- Funtime Star Flyer
- Mack Boomerang Splash
- S&S 4D Free Fly
- Zamperla Disk'o
- A water rapids or Splash Battle ride
- A family coaster
- Ferris wheel
- Children's land, with carousel

- A somewhat unrealistic major coaster

- An outdoor theater

- Twin drop towers

- Another major coaster, with indoor elements, that will run past the park's entrance

In addition, Six Flags promises an evening lights and fireworks show over the park.

Readers respond:

AJ Hummel: Looks like we've got six coasters (Mack PowerSplash, Intamin ZacSpin/S&S Free Spin, Gerstlauer Spinning Coaster, Zamperla Family Gravity Coaster, Rocky Mountain Construction wooden coaster (which looks very similar to Six Flags Great America's Goliath), and some unidentifiable coaster at the front of the park). In addition to what Robert listed, I also see a Mack Twist 'n' Splash, a set of Flying Scooters, and a couple spinner rides in the upper left (one looks like a tea cups, but I can't identify the other). Looks like a pretty nice park, though like the other Dubai projects I'll wait until it opens before deciding whether to add Dubai to my "to visit" list.

Interview with John Hallenbeck, General Manager of Motiongate Dubai
First published October 11, 2016

Something's about to happen in Dubai that's never before happened in the theme park industry. A new resort will open not just one, but three new parks in the space of just a couple months. Dubai Parks and Resorts will open the first of its three parks on Oct. 31 — the region's first Legoland theme park. Next month, the world's first Bollywood-themed park joins the mix. And in December, it's time for Motiongate Dubai, a movie-themed park that includes sections themed to Sony Pictures, Lionsgate, and DreamWorks.

I swapped emails earlier this month with Motiongate Dubai's General Manager, John Hallenbeck. That name might sound familiar to some long-time Theme Park Insider readers, as I interviewed him in Singapore in 2011 when he was the Vice President for Operations for Universal Studios Singapore and I was visiting the park for the world premiere of Transformers: The Ride 3D.

Now John's running the shop for a new movie-themed park on the other side of the continent. With opening day just a few weeks away, I asked him what fans can expect from Motiongate Dubai when it debuts.

"Motiongate Dubai is designed for everyone – families, couples, teens, adults and kids, so it really depends on the profile of our guests and the kind of experience they want to have," he said.

With three motion picture studio partners, plus a kid-focused land themed to The Smurfs, Motiongate Dubai can draw upon a deep collection of IP to mix a variety of ride systems and attraction types to appeal to a wide range of visitors.

"Families will enjoy all of the five rides and attractions in the Smurfs Village Zone, or the exciting water rapids ride River Expedition, inspired by Cloudy with a Chance of Meatballs in Sony Pictures Studios Zone," Hallenbeck said. "For those looking for thrill, we have five awesome roller coasters including Capitol Bullet Train, the first roller coaster inspired by The Hunger Games franchise in the Lionsgate Zone... or our fastest roller coaster in the park, Madagascar: Mad Pursuit in the DreamWorks Zone."

And not everything in the park is a ride, of course.

"Guests who enjoy live entertainment can watch our hip-hop live stage show, 'Step Up Dubai: All In!' which is inspired by that hit film franchise," Hallenbeck said. "All of our rides, attractions and entertainment are as equally enjoyable as the next experience, so guests are invited to 'play their role' and create their own cinematic adventure."

That "adventure" clearly is designed to appeal to fans who are used to the level of detail typically found in Disney and Universal theme parks, while offering them an experience that's different when compared with those parks.

"The theming [at Motiongate Dubai] is world-class, and puts guests right into the action," Hallenbeck said. "[A] unique element would definitely be the DreamWorks Zone, a completely indoor environment which takes guests through four immersive lands."

The indoor setting the DreamWorks pavilion is a plus considering the often harsh desert environment in the United Arab Emirates, which can make Orlando-style heat seem like a pleasant spring day.

"Motiongate Dubai has been designed to be a year-round destination, and the park's design incorporates cooling zones, air-conditioned queuing systems for all of our rides and attractions, shaded areas and landscaping," Hallenbeck said. "In fact, 21 of our 27 key rides and attractions are completely indoors – including the DreamWorks Zone, which is essentially a theme park within a theme park featuring 12 rides and attractions alone."

The Middle East hasn't traditionally offered much for theme park fans, but with Ferrari World in nearby Abu Dhabi and the recent opening of IMG Worlds of Adventure — not to mention a planned expansion of Dubai Parks & Resorts to include the region's first Six Flags park — the UAE is working to position itself not just as an alternative to Florida for European visitors, but as a leading destination for themed entertainment fans all over the world.

"Motiongate Dubai has over 50 nationalities working together which will enable us to offer a truly global experience for our guests from around the world," Hallenbeck said. "Dubai is a melting pot of cultures, and I'm proud to be part of such a rich and culturally diverse team."

Motiongate Dubai opens December 16. One-day tickets to Motiongate Dubai will cost AED330 (about US$89.95) and a three-day "All Parks Hopper" to Motiongate Dubai, Bollywood Parks

Dubai and Legoland Dubai will be AED870 (US$236.87), among other multi-day and annual pass options for the parks.

Readers respond:

grant crawford: I'm surprised the parks aren't a bit cheaper, but I guess they're primarily aimed at international guests with a bit more coin. I'd be keen to go there someday (been to Dubai before and it's a great place to visit), but there's many other places on the bucket list first. Maybe as a stopover

Rob McCullough: I worked with John during the opening of Islands of Adventure. He's a great leader, and a remarkably nice person. Motiongate Dubai sounds like an outstanding operation. Hope to get there someday.

Robert Niles: Here's some context for the prices. To go all the way to the top of the Burj Khalifa (the world's tallest building, located in Dubai) costs AED500. That's more than US$136 at today's exchange rate. For an elevator ride (with a helluva view, but still...).

You'll 'Marvel' at the Lack of Waiting in the World's Largest Indoor Theme Park
First published October 18, 2016, by Andy Farr

DUBAI — We all want that ultimate "Fastpass," the one that gives us exclusive access to the theme park with walk-ons to all rides, no queues for restaurants, no crowds to get in our way, the cost of this Fastpass? Apparently, it's 270AED ($72/£63) — the price of a standard entry ticket to IMG Worlds of Adventure on a Tuesday (plus flights and hotel, if you don't live locally, of course).

The world's largest indoor theme park had been open for five weeks when we visited, and the taxi driver told us we were the only fare he'd taken to the park since it opened. The first thing that strikes you as you arrive is that you've just travelled half an hour from the creek in Dubai to a construction site. The theme park is complete (though the adjacent cinema still is not open), but the site around it is just desert and road construction. Next, you will notice the vast car park — as big as any at Walt Disney World — but devoid of cars. We arrived just after opening and with tickets pre-booked and printed from the website, we walked straight into the reception area, through security with no bags to check, and then into the park.

The park has three themed lands and a central boulevard containing the Haunted Hotel walk-through attraction, plus shops and restaurants. In the park, you will find 12 rides, a 5D theatre, two play areas, a show and that walk-through. The park was open from 11am until 9pm on the day we visited.

Once inside the theme park we realised how empty it is. We walked along the boulevard towards the Haunted Hotel, and we're the only ones on the street.

The first of the three lands we visited was the Lost Valley, themed around dinosaurs. The area is gloomy and with minimal signage and with no crowd to follow, we walked up the exit to Predator, only to be told by staff to go round to the correct entrance. We did, and walked straight on to the Gerstlauer Euro-Fighter coaster. No waiting, get in the carriage, restraint pulled down, checked and off we go. Up at 90 degrees, over and down a short drop at 90 degrees, then round a few loops and turns, all over in less than a minute.

Our next ride was Velociraptor, a Mack Rides launch coaster. You load inside the theme park, but as the ride starts the doors to the outside open, the heat from the desert hits you, and you blast off onto the park's only ride that goes outside the building.

After that, we went on Forbidden Territory — which basically was Dinosaur from Disney's Animal Kingdom, with a slightly different story — and then finished the land with a ride on the Dino Carousel. Less than 30 minutes into our visit, and we've done four rides. So we're off to Marvel Zone.

Marvel Zone is a brighter area themed to a cityscape containing five Avengers-themed rides. Still no queues, as we walk on to

Avengers Flight of the Quinjets (think Disney's Astro Orbiter) and ride as a couple... with no one else aboard. Next, we go on Thor Thunder Spin, and the downside to an empty park arises. They need a minimum of 12 riders to operate this Top Spin ride, so we sit on the ride waiting for 10 minutes as attendants coax other guests to ride so we can start. After riding Thor, we have the longest wait of the day as we remain take a few pictures and a short video of the next group of riders on Thor before moving onto Avengers Battle of Ultron.

Battle of Ultron is another walk-on. We pause just to take a couple of photos of the queue. After that dark ride, trips on Spider-Man Doc-Ocks Revenge, a Mack Rides a spinning coaster, and Hulk Epsilon Base 3D, a 360-degree theater show, quickly follow, then we were off to Cartoon Network.

Cartoon Network is a more child-friendly area of the theme park, so it was a little busier, populated by families with small children. Still no queueing for rides, though, as we walk onto Adventure Time - The Ride of OOO with Finn & Jake, a overhead monorail that takes you on a short tour above this land. Then we went on The Amazing Ride of Gumball, a short ride with laser-pointer shooters, but unlike Disney World's Buzz Lightyear ride, you can't spin the car to get a better shot. After that, it was onwards to Ben 10 5D Hero Time. After a short wait for the current show to finish, we're into the large, empty theatre where we have the row to ourselves. No need to move all the way to the end. There's no possible way to fill in all this available space.

Once back to the central boulevard, we make our way to the Haunted Hotel, as it only opens after 1:30pm. It's well presented by actors in English, although not as creepy as the old House of Horror at Universal Studios Hollywood. Still, it's fun to watch a few locals jump and squeal, not knowing what to expect or from where.

So we've been in the park for less than three hours and we've done all the rides we want to do. (We've missed only The Powerpuff Girls – Mojo Jojo's Robot Rampage spinner ride.) What next?

You can't sit in the shade of a tree to relax and watch the word go by — there's no sun and there are very few guests. How about getting a good spot for the parade? There is no parade. Let's grab some photos with the characters in Marvel Zone? No characters to be seen. What about a show, you know, one like Beauty and the Beast or Indiana Jones at Disney? There's only one show with characters from LazyTown, and that doesn't appeal. OK, we'll look round the shops, then re-ride everything again.

At 4:30 pm, we've walked round the park at least three times. We've had enough of coasters for today, and we finally decide it's time to eat. There are plenty of choices: sit down, fast food carts, Arabic, Indian, Chinese, Burgers, hotdogs, pizzas, popcorn — all available with no queueing. We decide to sit in a tuk-tuk and have samosas. Food cost are on a par with the water parks in Dubai, 15AED – 25AED for water or soft drinks, around 30AED for snacks and +60AED for meals. As we eat our meal, we decide we've had enough for the day and phone the taxi to collect us... in 45 minutes outside the entrance plaza.

The real cost of the ultimate Fastpass at a park with few guests and unlimited rides? You get bored pretty quickly. There's no anticipation — no build up to the ride as you wait in the queue. The rides lose their value when obtained so easily.

IMG Worlds of Adventure may call itself a theme park, but just having the rights to and using IP does not a theme park make. Instead, here we get: staff, all in the same blue or orange polo shirts, wherever they were working, instead of costumes; no parades, shows or characters to promote the IP; and worst of all, no natural elements to add to the little amount of theming that exists — no trees and birds, no sunshine, no changing light from night to day. These elements help us 'live' in the environment we find ourselves in. But here, you always can see the roof over your head.

Marvel Zone and Lost Valley have great coasters that would be "A" rides at any theme park, but the whole park lacks elements that make it a memorable day out. Less than a week after visiting, our overriding memory is how empty the park was.

As reported on Theme Park Insider at the time of opening, the owners expect more than four million visitors in the park's first year. Whilst it's hard to estimate how many visitors were in the park during our visit, I'd reckon no more than 1,000. Maybe the park is busier at the weekends?

But it's never going to be the nearly 80,000 a week that would be required to get annual capacity up to four million. Now, add into the mix that three new theme parks will be opening very soon in Dubai, and that there are two well-established water parks all chasing the same tourists and local families, and I'd say the park would be closing for good after one season if it were anywhere else but Dubai.

Readers respond:

Robert Niles: Thanks for the trip report Andy! I think this illustrates why IP isn't everything in theme parks today, despite what many of us might be feeling. Context still matters. We want to visit themed environments, not just rides in a mall.

Now, part of the context that is missing here is a critical mass for themed entertainment in Dubai. In that respect, the new Dubai Parks and Resorts, along with Ferrari World in Abu Dhabi, might help IMG Worlds rather than hurt it. If, together, all of these attractions lure more theme park fans to the UAE, maybe those queue will start to fill.

But, please, not until I get the chance to go and get on everything with no wait! ;^)

Reid Loveland: Too much "blue sky"-ing by the people behind this theme park (as well as the others). No business wants to get started thinking business/attendance will be bad; every company wants to believe they are the best and customers will flock to their doors. But I see this happen all the time on a small scale in my town. Someone opens a shop and they are out of business less than a year alter because they had no customers. And the problem is these places don't research customer wants and needs, or perform critical feasibility studies on traffic flow and everything else that can affect them. And this theme park has done the same thing. Maybe the government of Dubai promised them thousands and thousands of guests everyday, but a good operational study might have shown them the truth. If they don't cut their hours and possibly close a few days a week, they will be losing money for their owners until Dubai gets more developed and starts bringing in more visitors who enjoy theme parks.

Rob McCullough: This is the second trip report I have read for this park today. Both say the same thing. The attractions are quality, but the overall feel of the place misses the mark. I was just looking over the website for the Bollywood park opening soon at Dubai Parks and Resorts. My mental image of being in a Bollywood movie is frenetic energy. Lots and lots and lots of people in a small area - in a good way. Imagine how weird that place will feel if it's not bustling. I hope they are all successful, but you gotta get people through the doors, and IMG Worlds of Adventure seems to have a long way to go to hit 80K a week.

Tony Perkins: The UAE has quite a few carcasses of failed amusement parks, and Ferrari World has been empty since it opened. It's not a surprise this one is empty as well. The major water parks do great in attendance (though the smaller water parks, such as Dreamland in Um Al Quwain, are dying). The price is too high except for local Emiratis and Western expats (and there's been an exodus of the latter in the past year with the drop in crude oil prices). Tourists come to the UAE for the lap of luxury, and this park isn't up to that market. Russian and Chinese oligarchs just won't be interested in this park.

The real test will be the three opening by Dubai Parks & Resorts in the next three months. It will be interesting, especially since they will be all outdoors. My prediction:

Legoland: Decently successful. Emiratis (and their maids) will bring their kids to the park regularly. Should do well with annual passes if they market to the locals heavily.

Bollywood: Major failure. After the curiosity factor wears out in a few weeks, it will be a ghost town. Priced way too high for South Asians, who mostly make peanuts in the UAE. Emiratis and expats will go once and done. The attractions don't seem to have much repeatability (shows and screens).

Motiongate: This is the make or break park for the whole venture. With the budget they have, I think they've done what they can to make this work (mix of indoor/outdoor attractions and various IPs) but I'm not sure it's enough. None of the IPs is a home run that would make it a sure-fire destination visit. I hope it succeeds but I got a bad feeling about this...

From an anonymous reader: I cannot say that I'm surprised that this park is empty. My opinion is it's location. Dubai residents and visitors do not match the amusement park demographic. And vice versa, the amusement park goers will not be traveling to Dubai - for many reasons such as costs and primarily culture. To echo what Alex posted - one curse word or touch of a stranger on the shoulder probably, would land you in jail. No thanks!

Disfan: It looks very sad, and reminds me of Las Vegas in the 90s, when they tried to open family friendly attractions like the MGM Grand Adventure Theme Park and attractions at the Luxor. They had some interesting attractions, but the theming and immersiveness was just not enough. This looking like rides inside a mall is an apt description. I think it's very hard to make an indoor theme park look like outside environments, you're always aware of the roof, even painting the roof like the sky is not enough. Also, I've heard that upscale clientele aren't as interested in theme parks, they're more interested in five star treatment.

THE REST OF THE STORIES

Disney Legend, Theme Park Hall of Famer Jack Lindquist Passes Away
First published February 28, 2016

Jack Lindquist, the former Disneyland President who created the Disney Dollar and the "I'm Going to Disneyland!" campaign, has died. He was 88.

Lindquist was named a Disney Legend for his leadership of the company's theme parks, and last fall was inducted into the amusement industry Hall of Fame at the IAAPA Attractions Expo in Orlando. Born March 15, 1927 in Chicago, Lindquist started working at Disneyland shortly after the park opened in 1955. Working his way up from an advertising manager, Lindquist pioneered some of the most influential practices and promotions in the entertainment industry, including off-site ticket sales and after-hours special events.

In 2013, Jack talked with Theme Park Insider about his career, including the development of Disney Dollars and the birth of the wildly successful "I'm going to Disneyland/Disney World" campaign, which earned the company an incomprehensible amount of free publicity over the years.

In November, the International Association of Amusement Parks and Attractions enshrined Lindquist in its Hall of Fame, recognizing not just his service to Disneyland and to the Disney theme parks worldwide, but also his influence on the promotion and operation of the entire theme park industry.

Readers respond:

From an anonymous reader: I don't know what's even more sad, the fact that we have lost such a creative mind, or that I never heard about this guy until just now after he died. :/ Well, either way, RIP, Mr. Lindquist. Tell Walt and Roy we said hi!

B Goodwin: When you look at a huge corporation like Disney, you generally only think of Walt, or Eisner, or Iger. But its the creativity of so many people, like Jack Lindquist, that have made the company as great as it is today, and helped set the bar so high for Themed entertainment. It's nice that Theme Park Insider takes the time to recognize this man and his peers, and their contribution to the parks. Rest in Peace, sir. For the Disney dollar that has sat in my wallet for so many years, and for all the additional amusement you have added to my favorite entertainment company, I thank you.

Theme Park Insider Interview with Disney's Jack Lindquist
First published August 7, 2013

Many theme park fans might know Jack Lindquist as the first president of Disneyland, a role he played from 1990 to his retirement in 1993. But Jack started working at Disneyland a few months after the park opened in 1955. Along the way, he developed or helped develop many of the practices and promotions that became Disney and theme park industry standards, including off-site ticket sales and after-hours special events. He even invented the Disney Dollar!

It's important for theme park fans to recognize that theme parks operate they way that they do today not by some accident, but because innovative leaders such as Jack Lindquist figured out how to make them work. Jack's written about his years working for Disney in his book, In Service To The Mouse: My Unexpected Journey to Becoming Disneyland's First President, and he spoke with us this week.

Like a great manager, Jack gives much credit to the cast members he worked with over the years, but Jack's willingness to embrace innovation surely helped establish Disney as the industry leader in theme parks for his generation, as well as for the next. Disney honored Jack as a Disney Legend in 1994, and, I hope, IAAPA one day will honor him with a spot in its theme park industry Hall of Fame.

Robert: You started at Disneyland as its advertising manager, just a few months after the park opened in 1955. Obviously, Walt himself helped sell America on Disneyland with his television show. But getting people from dreaming about a Disney theme park trip to actually buying their tickets takes a lot of additional work. Along the way, you developed or helped develop many of the ways of doing that: off-site sales of tickets, special events, giveaways, even the "I'm going to Disneyland" commercials. How were you able to develop so many promotions that not only worked, but became standards for other companies to follow and imitate?

Jack: I think it was I continually tried to find ideas that were different, that hadn't been done, that needed to be done, and to design promotions and ad campaigns around that. One of the best things we had going in the very early days of Disneyland was ignorance. We didn't know we couldn't do something, but we knew it had to be done, so we just went ahead and did it. There were no books to go by; there had never been a project like this before. So you just had to improvise, be intuitive. I just did what was necessary.

That's how the whole thing with the New Year's Eve party, with the advance sale of tickets, came about. I knew that we couldn't fill a New Year's Eve party, and sell 5-6,000 tickets at a minimum, just by having people come to a box office in Anaheim. So we started talking to stores. Pretty soon we had 8-10 locations, from Long

Beach to Pasadena to Westwood to Newport Beach, where people could get tickets, in advance, and not have to drive to Anaheim. And it worked. We sold about 5,000 tickets away from the park, and about 3,500 tickets at the park. And we didn't pay any commissions to any of those outlets. As I told [them], 'I'll just drive people into your store. If they buy something [else], good. I can't promise you that, but they'll be there, and it's up to you to capture while they're there.'

On "I'm going to Disneyland!"

Jack: Michael Eisner and [his wife] Jane were having dinner at the Plaza Inn on the night that they opened Star Tours, and they were hosting Dick Rutan and Jeana Yeager, who'd just flown around the world in that small plane. Jane Eisner said, 'My gosh, you folks have flown around the world nonstop, what are you going to do next?' And [Jeana] said, 'We're going to Disneyland!' Jane turned to Michael and said, 'That's a good phrase, remember it.'

After dinner, Michael came outside and found me and Tom Elrod, the VP of marketing at Walt Disney World. So Tom and I talked about we could use [the line.] We said there's a Super Bowl game in about three weeks: Denver versus the New York Giants, at the Rose Bowl in Pasadena. What if we had the MVP from that game, right at the end of the game, on the field, say 'I'm going to Disney World! I'm going to Disneyland!' Can we make that happen?

We went to the NFL, went to NBC, and then we talked about who would be the MVP. We decided that the quarterbacks would be the best bet. So we went to Phil Simms and John Elway and their agents and started negotiating. We signed both of them, and as it worked out, Phil Simms was the MVP. We shot it as soon as the game ended, when they were on the field. And overnight, we got it to the Today Show, where we bought time for the next morning, as well as on Good Morning America and the CBS Morning News. And the thing that happened, it got picked up and ran on news shows all over the country, gratis.

Then we went to the World Series and did the same thing. We went to the Indianapolis 500. We went to the NBA Finals. People expected those commercials immediately following a major sporting event. And it all came from remarks that a young lady made to Jane Eisner. Jane deserves all the credit for recognizing that was a great advertising line.

Robert: Many fans might know you just as the first president of Disneyland, but you worked on projects in Florida, too, including the development of Epcot. In your book, you've got some great stories about trying to recruit nations to become part of World Showcase — stories that make me wonder how anyone ever gets anything done in international diplomacy. What's your favorite memory from the Epcot project?

Jack: There are so many, but probably my favorite was the time we spent in Iran with the Shah. It was exactly a year before the overthrow of his regime. We spent five weeks there. He was very gracious; we met with him, his wife and his top leaders. I have no idea how ruthless he may have been as the ruler of that country. You felt an undercurrent — there were things happening, you didn't know what — you just felt it. The thing [the Shah] was most impressed with, though, the thing he kept referring over and over to us, was that when he took the throne after World War II, 98 percent of his people were illiterate. And just that year, reports show that over 52 percent of his people could read and write. He was so proud that 50,000 young Iranians were going, at the government's expense, to universities all over the world, and that they would come back and be the leaders of Iran in the 21st century.

Robert: Well, he was right.

Jack: Yeah, but he didn't see that side. World Showcase was an interesting project. For three years, I traveled over 300,000 miles a year, and visited 43 different countries.

Robert: Later in the 1980s, you pulled off some epic giveaway promotions, for Disneyland's 30th and 35th birthdays. Everything from free tickets to cars. What made you develop those promotions, and why don't we see parks giving away stuff like that anymore?

Jack: I don't know! [Laughs] I know why we did it, though. In 1985, that followed the Olympics in Los Angeles, which everyone predicted would be a boom for tourism, and turned out was a bust. The Olympics was a spectacular show, but it didn't drive hotel occupancy, theme park visitation or anything that we expected. So we were coming off about 9.2 million attendance for 1984, and we needed something to really highlight '85. I was sitting around thinking, 'Well, it'll be our 30th anniversary." Well, nobody celebrated a 30th of anything, but I said, 'Why not?' So I got started thinking that it's our birthday, but I want to give presents to our guests. I talked with a people inside and outside of the company, and the one single thing [people wanted] was automobiles. We went to General Motors, which was one of our new lessees at Epcot Center, and we worked out a deal with them. We gave away that year 106 General Motors cars, from Chevrolets to Cadillacs.

We started with every 30th person won something, then every 300th, 3,000th, 30,000th, 300,000th, and three millionth. In my original memo to [then-CEO] Ron [Miller], I said that if we don't do 12 million people between Jan. 1, 1985 and Dec. 31, 1985, I'll resign. So he'll win if we lose. And we did 12,040,000 people.

It worked. But it took everyone in the park to make it work. We totally computerized our entire front gate. We had Price Waterhouse underwrite the program, to give it the credibility it needed. We had to abide by all the federal and state regulations for lotteries and so forth. We had several hundred people win who never attended the park. We had a computerized turnstile set up [over by the kennel]. They went through it just the same as if they bought a ticket and went through the front gate, and if it hit one of those numbers, they won something. I think we had four of those people win cars, who never went into the park.

Robert: So Disney Dollars were your idea? How did you make that happen?

Jack: I was flying back from a trip to Europe, and you've got 11 hours of time to kill. I was going through my change, and there were Francs, and Deutsch Marks, and Pounds, and so forth. And I thought, you know a lot of these countries we just visited, we do more people per year than their population. So why can't we have a currency?

This was not some cheap promotion thing. I wanted a real currency. So we went to the Secret Service and we built in all the safeguards for counterfeiting. It was an expensive project, but we printed the money, and we introduced it in May 1985. I think we had 40 or 50 people standing in line, overnight, at the box office to be the first people to purchase Disney Dollars. One man, the first morning, bought $10,000 worth.

I got a call about two weeks later from the Kellogg's people. They'd heard about Disney Dollars and were interested in talking with us about putting a Disney Dollar in every box of corn flakes. They came to California, we had a meeting, and I said, 'How many boxes of corn flakes in a month are we talking about?' And he said, 'About a million and a half.' I said, 'I'm very interested.'

Everything went fine until he said 'What's the discount?' And I said, 'There is no discount.' He said, 'You don't understand. We're going to use a million and a half Disney Dollars. What's it going to cost us?' And I said, 'A million and a half dollars.'

I told him, 'I'll make you a deal. You go to the U.S. Treasury and tell them you're going to put a dollar in every box of Kellogg's. I will give you the same discount you get from them.' We never saw them again.

I think that was the success of it. It wasn't just a promotional dollar. It was a Disney Dollar. You can go into a Disney park today, take your old Disney Dollar to the box office, and get a [U.S.] dollar for it. The last report I got was in 1996 from the head of finance in Florida who told me that, at that time, there was about $135 million in Disney Dollars that were out. So I said, 'Good, [with that] I just built Indiana Jones at Disneyland!' [Laughs]

Robert: You were one of the first — if not the first — advocate inside the company for building a second gate in Anaheim. What was your involvement in that effort over the years?

Jack: I was the guy on the soapbox, starting in 1982, for a second gate at Disneyland. You can keep adding new attractions to the park, but you need to do something like Florida did with Epcot Center, a whole new park, something you can really make a fuss about, more than any new attraction.

Disneyland was an aging property. A second gate was the most practical way to extend length of stay — and that's the basis for any second gate. So instead of a one, one-and-a-half day visit, you're going to stay three days. I felt that's exactly what we needed in California. I fought for that from 1982 until I retired, when Michael bought off on the concept of the second gate. I didn't know [then] exactly what it was going to be, and it turned out to be California Adventure, which wasn't a good park when it opened. But in 2012, when they opened Cars Land, now it's a good park.

A second park has to be real, or perceived, to be equal to the first park. Epcot certainly was. California Adventure wasn't when it opened. I think during the construction of California Adventure, someone needed to go up to Michael and say, 'If you're not going to spend at least a couple hundred million more dollars, at least, to make California Adventure a park that can be perceived as equal to Disneyland, leave it a parking lot.'

Michael changed over the years. I enjoyed very much working with Michael from 1984 to 1993, and that's because he had Frank Wells. They were a great team. When we lost Frank, I think Michael really lost more than he could cope with.

Robert: What's your advice to anyone getting into this industry today? What does a newcomer to this business need to know in order to have the same kind of success that you enjoyed during your career?

Jack: You gotta like it. You gotta like it from the first time you see it. Then stick with it — you never know what's going to happen.

I was very happy with the job I had for an ad agency, but I saw Disneyland, in May 1955, two months before it opened. Just looking at it, I fell in love with it. I had the chance to go to work there, and I jumped at it. I don't know why. It didn't make economic sense or geographic sense. I lived in Burbank. So for [the first] six months, I drove from Burbank to Anaheim, without a freeway.

Learn everything you can. I never thought that marketing was the most important thing in the world. It isn't. It's everything working together. It's operations. It's maintenance. It's finance. It's legal. And today, all of those things are a lot more important than they were in 1955. It's the whole. Learn everything you can about every facet of how the park works.

Some of the most popular articles we publish on Theme Park Insider provide advice on getting the most for your money when you visit a park. But not all consumer advice has to be about big-ticket items such as airfares and hotel stays.

How to Save a Couple Bucks on a Disneyland Corn Dog
First published January 23, 2016

Many theme park fans consider a stop at Main Street's Little Red Wagon for a corn dog as important a part of a Disneyland visit as a trip on Pirates of the Caribbean or watching the fireworks show at the end of the day.

But if you pause at the $8.75 price tag, we've got an insider tip for you on how to save a couple bucks on that Disneyland corn dog.

The corn dogs at the Little Red Wagon are freshly dipped in batter and fried instead of frozen in advance and stored in a warehouse, elevating these rather humble dogs to something fans crave long after returning home. Disney several years ago famously ditched their all-beef hot dogs for a beef-and-chicken mix, but under this crispy and ever-so-lightly-sweet cornbread shell, they still taste fantastic.

But Disney sells you more than just a freshly-dipped corn dog for that $8.75. It includes a "small bag of chips," as well, with the option of substituting a bag of apple slices, instead. Yet here's the third option that Disney doesn't tell you about — you can choose neither.

Just tell the host or hostess taking your order that you would prefer not have the chips or the apple slices, and the host will knock the price of the corn dog down to $6.50. That's a $2.25 discount, simply by foregoing a small bag of Lay's potato chips.

This tip works at any Disney food cart or counter-service restaurant that bundles chips or fruit with the main item you are ordering. If you don't really want the side item, just say so, and enjoy a discount. You'll also save calories by not guilt-eating an accompaniment you didn't want or need, anyway, just because you paid for it.

Readers add:

From an anonymous reader: Also, if you have an annual pass, the Stage Door Cafe, which also serves the same corn dog, will apply the discount!

And some stories... well, some stories are just bizarre.

Dopey Falls During Fantasmic Mishap at Walt Disney World
First published August 7, 2016

A slip led to a scary moment during tonight's performance of Fantasmic! at Disney's Hollywood Studios in Florida.

Dopey slipped during the show's finale, falling under the railing on the top level of the steamboat down onto the level below. In falling, Dopey landed on Goofy, who broke the Snow White character's fall. A fan captured the incident and uploaded it the video, where it's gone viral.

Obviously, the first concern is for the health of both character performers — not just Dopey for falling several feet but also for Goofy having to take the force of Dopey's fall. Fortunately, Goofy's presence helped slow Dopey and take some of the force of the fall, not to mention keeping Dopey from falling into the water. But I can't imagine what it would be like to be performing in full character head and suit and to have another character drop on your back unexpectedly. I also can't imagine that this incident won't prompt an enormous amount of discussion within Disney, as whatever the fall protection plan on the Fantasmic! riverboat is clearly didn't get the job done tonight.

The performer playing Chip immediately went to Dopey's assistance, and you can see in the video Dopey making a hand signal to Chip. Initial reports on social media said that both actors involved escaped immediate injury. They were checked at the scene by paramedics and released.

Readers respond:

grant crawford: I'm glad there appear to be no injuries and there are obvious safety concerns here, he came very close to going over the lower rail.

I can't help but to see the funny side though. It had to be Dopey, didn't it? Did Doc run right up to help too? And was Chip just checking if Dopey had any acorns in his pockets? I can imagine Grumpy will be the occupational health and safety rep to take this to management. Sorry, my bad imagination and worse humour getting away with me.

Melissa Donahue: Although Dopey had a start value of 15.8, he managed to salvage a yellow score thanks to Goofy. I can't stop laughing out loud when I watch this video, but all kidding aside, I'm relieved to hear that no one was seriously injured.

From an anonymous reader: I felt really bad for chuckling a bit. I'm not sure why watching someone else fall is funny - it shouldn't be. But, America's Funniest Home Videos made a whole show out of it. But, they all stayed focused - the show must go on.

Dopey just missed falling in the water. Goofy was definitely in the right spot to save him. I think had he gone in the water its more likely it would have been serious. Injury by the boat movement and the weight of that costume wet. Thankful it was not any worse and I'll be watching for the updated railing when I go in three weeks.

Robert Niles: I'm guessing that you could fix this with a third crossbar at shoe level, or by moving the rail in from the edge of the platform. That's the serious answer. The easy, sarcastic one is to never put Dopey on the upper deck. Keep him close to the ground, where he can't hurt himself, anyone or anything. And don't give him anything to wave, either. We know his track record.

From an anonymous reader: After 18 years of performance and probably 5-7000 shows, I am sure this isn't the first thing to go wrong. Weird stuff happens on stage and in the rest of the world. Learn from the mistake, add some additional safety measures, if necessary take a couple days off in a couple of weeks to make more permanent changes and let the show go on. While prepping the changes, review the emergency plans, especially for dwarf overboard, starboard side.

THE BEST OF 2016

Theme Park Insider Award Winners

Every year on the Fourth of July holiday, Theme Park Insider honors our readers' favorite theme park hotels, restaurants, and attractions with our Theme Park Insider Awards. The winners are the locations in each category with the highest average reader rating and a minimum number of ratings overall. Attractions that opened officially to the public at major theme parks between July 1, 2015 and June 30, 2016 were eligible in the Best New Attraction categories. Let's get to the honors!

Best New Attraction: *Pirates of the Caribbean Battle for the Sunken Treasure, Shanghai Disneyland*

The world's newest major theme park wins our award this year for Best New Attraction. Shanghai Disneyland's version of Pirates of the Caribbean refreshes the wildly popular franchise with a new ride system and aggressive use of projection mapping and screens with the traditional animatronics to create a jaw-dropping adventure.

Previous winners: Justice League Battle for Metropolis [2015], Banshee [2014], Mystic Manor [2013], Transformers The Ride [2012], Star Tours The Adventures Continue [2011], Harry Potter and the Forbidden Journey [2010], Manta [2009], The Simpsons Ride [2008], Mystery Mine [2007], Expedition Everest [2006]

Best New Show: *Frozen Live at the Hyperion, Disney California Adventure*

Filled with visually stunning moments that accentuate the animated hit's beloved score, this version of Frozen already has become a must-see at the Disneyland Resort.

Best New Roller Coaster: *Mako, SeaWorld Orlando*

SeaWorld's latest Bolliger & Mabillard masterpiece is now Orlando's tallest and fastest roller coaster. The B&M hyper might be Theme Park Insider's favorite roller coaster model, and Mako's well on its way to the top of our coaster rankings.

Previous winner: Thunderbird [2015]

Best Quick-Service Restaurant: *The Three Broomsticks, Universal Studios Hollywood*

Our winner in this category is a new restaurant this year — the dining hall in Universal Studios Hollywood's recently opened Wizarding World of Harry Potter. Featuring not only favorites from Orlando's original but also some meals from last year's winner, The Leaky Cauldron, Hollywood's The Three Broomsticks offers more than enough great options to keep wizards and witches coming back again and again.

Previous winners: The Leaky Cauldron [2015], Miss Lillian's Chicken House [2014]

Best Table-Service Restaurant: *Magellan's, Tokyo DisneySea*

This Tokyo DisneySea restaurant wins its first Theme Park Insider Award, after years of knocking on the door. Located in the heart of the Mysterious Island Citadel, Magellan's is the headquarters of the Society of Explorers and Adventurers — a favorite franchise of Theme Park Insider readers.

Previous winners: Monsieur Paul [2015], S.S. Columbia Dining

Room [2013-2014], Bistro De Paris [2010-2012], Les Chefs de France [2009], Mythos Restaurant [2003-2008], Blue Bayou Restaurant [2002]

Best Hotel Restaurant: *Victoria and Albert's, Disney's Grand Floridian Resort and Spa, Walt Disney World*

Walt Disney World's most acclaimed restaurant wins this honor for the second year in a row.

Previous winner: Victoria and Albert's [2015]

Best Hotel: *Universal's Portofino Bay Hotel, Universal Orlando Resort*

Universal Orlando's flagship hotel captures our Theme Park Insider Award for the fourth year in row and the sixth overall. The exemplary service and accommodations would place the Portofino Bay near the top of our rankings by themselves, but the location and free Universal Express service for guests pushes the hotel to the very top.

Previous winners: Universal's Portofino Bay Hotel [2002, 2009, 2013-2015], Disney's Grand Californian Hotel [2003-2004, 2011-2012], Disney's Wilderness Lodge [2010], Disney's Animal Kingdom Lodge [2005-2006, 2008], Disney's Polynesian Resort [2007]

Best Theme Park: *Tokyo DisneySea*

Tokyo DisneySea wins our top honor for the fifth year in a row and the sixth time overall. But Disney's new Shanghai park is off to a strong start and continued expansion at the Universal Orlando Resort mean that theme park fans around the world are enjoying a resurgence of high quality in the theme park business. That's great news for fans, and something to look forward to seeing more of in the years to come.

Previous winners: Tokyo DisneySea [2005, 2012-2015], Universal's Islands of Adventure [2002-2004, 2010-2011], Disneyland [2008-2009], Busch Gardens Williamsburg [2006-2007]

Congratulations to all the winners!

Ranking the Class of 2016

The Top 10 Best New Attractions of the Year

1. Pirates of the Caribbean Battle for the Sunken Treasure, Shanghai Disneyland: Our winner of the Theme Park Insider Award for Best New Attraction of the year.

2. Harry Potter and the Forbidden Journey, Universal Studios Hollywood: "Universal's third installation of this tour through Hogwarts Castle might be its best yet, keeping Japan's 3D enhancements and adding an extra scene with Dementors. But the addition of a personal fan blowing onto each ride also helps reduce the nausea that some riders experienced on this heels-over-head thrill ride."

3. Frozen - Live at the Hyperion, Disney's California Adventure: "Overall, this new musical based on Disney's Academy Award-winning animated feature is a visual delight, demanding repeat viewings to catch all the detail. No, Frozen won't offer Aladdin's ever-changing line-up of pop culture one-liners. But with engaging images, impressive stagecraft and that wonderful music, Disney's Frozen - Live at the Hyperion feels just like what Olaf ordered - a nice warm hug."

4. Mako, SeaWorld Orlando: "At 200 feet tall Mako does not tower above other hyper coasters on the planet, however that does not prevent it from being an outstanding ride. Riders in the front of the train experience 'ejector' air time on each hill through the break run, while the riders in the back enjoy intense 'floater' air time and more extreme G forces. Mako perfectly employs what hyper coasters are all about — speed and air time — while adding great theming and a message about the importance of conservation for sharks as only SeaWorld can do."

5. TRON Lightcycle Power Run, Shanghai Disneyland: "Even if you couldn't care less for the movie franchise, this is a guaranteed hit. The idea is that we are being scanned into the game world portrayed in the movies, where we will race in high-speed lightcycles. Disney claims it is one of the fastest coasters in any of its parks, and it does feel that way. Even without any loops and twists, the speed is what guarantees the thrill factor here, combined with the uniqueness of riding a roller coaster on a motorbike and, once again, its great theming."

6. *Incredible Hulk Coaster, Universal's Islands of Adventure*: "What Universal did was take a great ride, and make it almost perfect. Probably the most themed large roller coaster out there, it's beautiful queue and unbelievable launch makes this newly rebuilt ride much more unique than other coasters. Like any other looping Bolliger & Mabillard coaster, this ride is packed with intensity and inversions that no other coaster can match. And although the wait time is pretty long, its two-minute-and-15-seconds ride time never will disappoint."

7. *Lightning Rod, Dollywood*: "The world's first launched wooden roller coaster, the $22 million Lightning Rod might be one of the best coasters in America. No other roller coaster so ruthless in its onslaught of airtime (that quadruple-down is perfect). Nearly every element provides insane airtime, and it also includes good theming and a beautiful environment."

8. *Jurassic Park The Flying Dinosaur, Universal Studios Japan*: "The park's fifth roller coaster, at 3,688 feet long, Jurassic Park The Flying Dinosaur is the world's longest Bolliger & Mabillard flying coaster, offering even more of the smooth exhilaration that B&M Flyers are known for, along with some great aerial views of the park."

9. *The New Revolution, Six Flags Magic Mountain*: "If you've been wondering when the theme park industry would develop a fresh, new type of ride — it's here. Many of us have fallen into the habit of always looking to Disney and Universal for industry advances. But after enjoying Six Flags' Theme Park Insider Award-winning Justice League Battle for Metropolis last year, which melded interactive gameplay with a 3D motion-base ride, and

experiencing The New Revolution this year, here's a crazy idea — the biggest innovator in theme parks today might just be Six Flags."

10. The Walking Dead, Universal Studios Hollywood: "Universal built The Walking Dead Attraction for its daytime audience, and the focus here is on detail and creating a richly immersive environment inspired by the show. Someone who's not a Walking Dead fan can push through and appreciate the impressive visuals in the burning cabin and prison scenes before hightailing it through the gore at the end. But a Walking Dead fan could easily spend hours walking through again and again, trying to pick up all the detail Universal has packed into this attraction."

Other Commendable New Attractions

Special Effects Show, Universal Studios Hollywood: The latest update of Universal's live show that illustrates the techniques and technology behind movie-making.

Valravn, Cedar Point: Bolliger & Mabillard's 100th roller coaster is the world's tallest, fastest and longest dive coaster.

Galactica, Alton Towers: A virtual reality overlay of the park's AIR coaster.

Star Wars A Galactic Spectacular, Disney's Hollywood Studios: A new night-time show, with fireworks, projection mapping and film clips from the Star Wars movies.

Buzz Lightyear Planet Rescue, Shanghai Disneyland: The latest, plussed installation of Disney's popular Toy Story-themed shooter ride.

Soarin' Around the World, Epcot, Disney's California Adventure, Shanghai Disneyland (as *Soaring Over the Horizon*): A new version of Disney's flying theater show takes us out of California and to new sights around the world, with different final scenes at each park.

Skull Island Reign of Kong, Universal's Islands of Adventure: A plussed version of Universal Studios Hollywood's King King

360/3D, adding a new Kong animatronic in the finale.

Ninjago The Ride, Legoland California: The world's first "weaponless" shooter ride — you use your hands to perform "Spinjitzu" and launch fireballs and ice blasts at your targets.

Frozen Ever After, Epcot: A Frozen-themed retheme of the Norway pavilion's Maelstrom boat ride features next-gen animatronics and those wildly popular songs from the movie.

Cobra's Curse, Busch Gardens Tampa: A Mack family spinning coaster with a vertical lift that puts you face to face with the Cobra King.

Also Pretty Good...

Luigi's Rollickin' Roadsters, Disney's California Adventure: Disney's first next-generation trackless ride in the United States replaces Luigi's flying tires with a ride in line-dancing cars.

Voyage to the Crystal Grotto, Shanghai Disneyland: A slow boat ride past static characters from Disney's animated films.

The Joker, Six Flags Great Adventure: An S&S Free Fly coaster.

Roaring Rapids, Shanghai Disneyland: A river rapids ride with an unique whirlpool effect... and a giant reptilian monster.

Not Enough Votes Yet to Rank

The rest of *Shanghai Disneyland*.

Benno's Great Race, Ferrari World Abu Dhabi: An interactive dark ride through the Italian countryside.

Flying Aces, Ferrari World Abu Dhabi: A 206-foot Intamin coaster that simulates a biplane flight with the world's largest loop.

Mickey and the Magician, Walt Disney Studios Park: A new musical stage show featuring songs from classic Disney films, replacing Animagique.

The Muppets Present Great Moments in American History, Walt Disney World's Magic Kingdom: The Muppets present their irreverent take on the story of America's founding, on the street in front of the Hall of Presidents. Two shows alternate, about the Declaration of Independence and the ride of Paul Revere.

Once Upon a Time, Walt Disney World's Magic Kingdom: A new nighttime projection mapping show on Cinderella Castle, narrated by Mrs. Potts from Beauty and the Beast, who tells "bedtime stories" with scenes from Disney's animated films.

Out of the Shadow Land, Tokyo DisneySea: A new live musical, the original story follows a shy girl as she develops the self-confidence to escape the evil shadow land in which she's been lost.

Theme Park Insider invites readers to rate and review all the attractions, restaurants, and hotels listed on our website. Visit www.themeparkinsider.com/reviews to get started!

2016's "Must Do" at the World's Top Theme Parks

Based upon our readers' ratings from the past year, here are the attractions and restaurants we recommend that you do not miss when you visit these popular theme parks in the next year. Visit www.themeparkinsider.com/reviews for complete descriptions and up-to-date listings for all these and other attractions, restaurants, and hotels in these resorts.

Please also visit www.themeparkinsider.com/plan for advice on planning your trip to any of these parks and then read www.themeparkinsider.com/flume/201610/5309 for our advice on how to reduce your wait times by using these parks' line-skipping alternatives.

Walt Disney World's Magic Kingdom

Rides

- *Splash Mountain* (Flume Ride, Frontierland, 40 inches to ride):

- *Haunted Mansion* (Indoor Track Ride, Liberty Square)

- *Tomorrowland Transit Authority PeopleMover* (Track Ride, Tomorrowland)
- *Big Thunder Mountain Railroad* (Roller Coaster, Frontierland, 40 inches to ride)

Shows

- *Festival of Fantasy* (Parade, Main Street USA)
- *Wishes* (Fireworks, Main Street USA)

Restaurants

- *Be Our Guest* (Quick Service Breakfast and Lunch, Table Service Dinner, Fantasyland)
- *Cinderella's Royal Table* (Character Meal, Fantasyland)

Epcot

Attractions

- *Impressions de France* (Movie, World Showcase - France)
- *Soarin' Around the World* (Flying Theater, Future World - The Land , 40 inches to ride)
- *Spaceship Earth* (Indoor Track Ride, Future World - Spaceship Earth)
- *The American Adventure* (Animatronic Show, World Showcase - American Adventure)
- *IllumiNations: Reflections of Earth* (Fireworks, World Showcase)

Table Service Restaurants

- *Monsieur Paul* (World Showcase - France)
- *Via Napoli* (World Showcase - Italy)
- *Le Cellier Steakhouse* (World Showcase - Canada)

Quick Service Restaurants

- *Kringla Bakeri Og Kafe* (World Showcase - Norway)
- *Les Halles Boulangerie and Patisserie* (World Showcase - France)

Disney's Hollywood Studios

Rides

- *Twilight Zone Tower of Terror* (Drop Tower, Sunset Boulevard, 40 inches to ride)
- *Rock 'n' Roller Coaster* (Roller Coaster, Sunset Boulevard, 48 inches to ride)
- *Toy Story Midway Mania* (Shooter Ride, Pixar Place)
- *Star Tours: The Adventures Continue* (Motion Base Show, Echo Lake, 40 inches to ride)

Show

- *Fantasmic!* (Outdoor Show, Sunset Boulevard)

Restaurant

- *The Hollywood Brown Derby* (Table Service, Hollywood Boulevard):

Disney's Animal Kingdom

Attractions

- *Kilimanjaro Safaris* (Narrated Ride, Africa)
- *Expedition Everest* (Roller Coaster, Asia, 44 inches to ride)
- *Festival of the Lion King* (Live Musical Show, Africa)
- *Finding Nemo - The Musical* (Live Musical Show, Dinoland USA)

- *Maharajah Jungle Trek* (Walk-Through Exhibit, Asia)
- Though they were not open yet at press time, we suggest checking out the new *Rivers of Light* nighttime show and the *Pandora: World of Avatar* land when they open in 2017.

Restaurants

- *Tiffins* (Table Service, Discovery Island)
- *Flame Tree Barbecue* (Quick Service, Discovery Island)

Universal Studios Florida

Attractions

- *Harry Potter and the Escape from Gringotts* (Motion Base Ride, The Wizarding World of Harry Potter - Diagon Alley, 42 inches to ride)

- *Revenge of the Mummy* (Roller Coaster, New York, 48 inches to ride)

- *Universal Horror Make-up Show* (Live Theater Show, Hollywood)

- *Men In Black Alien Attack* (Shooter Ride, World Expo, 42 inches to ride)

- *Transformers The Ride 3D* (Motion Base Ride, New York, 40 inches to ride)

- *Hogwarts Express* (Track Ride, The Wizarding World of Harry Potter - Diagon Alley. Leave this attraction for last, as it will carry you to the Islands of Adventure park next door. A Park to Park ticket is required to ride.)

Restaurants

- *The Leaky Cauldron* (Quick Service, The Wizarding World of Harry Potter - Diagon Alley)

- *Cafe La Bamba* (Character Meal, Hollywood)

Universal Orlando's Islands of Adventure

Attractions

- *The Amazing Adventures of Spider-Man* (Motion Base Ride, Marvel Super Hero Island, 40 inches to ride)

- *Incredible Hulk Coaster* (Roller Coaster, Marvel Super Hero Island, 54 inches to ride)

- *Harry Potter and the Forbidden Journey* (Motion Base Ride, The Wizarding World of Harry Potter, 48 inches to ride)

- *Hogwarts Express* (Track Ride, The Wizarding World of Harry Potter. Same deal as above. You will exit back at Universal Studios Florida. Park to Park ticket required.)

Restaurants

- *Mythos Restaurant* (Table Service, The Lost Continent)

- *The Three Broomsticks* (Quick Service, The Wizarding World of Harry Potter)

Disneyland

Rides

- *Pirates of the Caribbean* (Indoor Boat Ride, New Orleans Square)

- *Indiana Jones Adventure* (Motion Base Ride, Adventureland, 46 inches to ride)

- *Big Thunder Mountain Railroad* (Roller Coaster, Frontierland, 40 inches to ride)

- *Space Mountain* (Roller Coaster, Tomorrowland, 40 inches to ride)

Shows

- *Fantasy Faire Royal Theatre* (Live Theater Show, Fantasyland)
- *Fantasmic!* (Outdoor Show, Frontierland)

Restaurants

- *Carnation Cafe* (Table Service, Main Street USA)
- *Cafe Orleans* (Table Service, New Orleans Square)

Disney California Adventure

Rides

- *Radiator Springs Racers* (Track Ride, Cars Land, 40 inches to ride)
- *California Screamin'* (Roller Coaster, Paradise Pier, 48 inches to ride)
- *Toy Story Midway Mania* (Shooter Ride, Paradise Pier)
- We expect that *Guardians of the Galaxy Mission Breakout*, the replacement for the Twilight Zone Tower of Terror, also might become a "Must Do" at Disney California Adventure in 2017.

Shows

- *Frozen - Live at the Hyperion* (Live Musical Show, Hollywood Land)
- *World of Color* (Outdoor Show, Paradise Pier)
- *Animation Academy* (Instructional Show, Disney Animation Pavilion, Hollywood Land)

Restaurants

- *Carthay Circle Restaurant* (Table Service, Buena Vista Street)

- *Cove Bar* (Table Service, Paradise Pier)

Visit www.themeparkinsider.com/reviews for complete descriptions and reader reviews of all these locations and many others, at more than 50 major theme parks around the world.

A LOOK TOWARD 2017

Walt Disney World next year will open its most ambitious theme park land to date. **Pandora — The World of Avatar** will bring James Cameron's 3D aliens-vs.-developers film to life in Disney's Animal Kingdom. Visitors will walk under floating mountains, ride with Mountain Banshees and float through a bioluminescent rainforest in the new land, which is scheduled to open sometime in the middle of 2017.

The land will feature two attractions: Flight of Passage and the Na'vi River Journey. The first is a "flying theater"-type attraction and the second a classic indoor boat ride. We were leaked the blueprints for the Flight of Passage show building back in 2013, before the ride — or the land — had an official name.

First Look at the Blueprints for Walt Disney World's Avatar 3D Attraction

First published November 30, 2013

Despite what you might have heard about Disney's future theme park attraction plans, the Avatar "World of Pandora" land at Disney's Animal Kingdom at the Walt Disney World Resort remains good to go, and we've seen the plans that prove it.

Disney's scheduled the first phase of Pandora to open in 2017, and based on the designs we've seen, we believe that phase will include the "Soarin'"-style 3D movie attraction.

Design plans for that attraction call for a massive, five- to six-story theater building, which will top out somewhere around 80 feet. The building will include four show theaters, which will radiate from a central hub from where visitors will load into the theaters.

Two of the four theaters will be ADA-compatible (more about that in a minute), and plans show three ride levels in the show building. The indoor portion of the queue will snake through a shorter building to the side of the main theater building. Just as the queue enters the theater building, the queue will split, and visitors will be sent onto one of two ramps. The left ramp will descend slightly to the first show level, while the right ramp will ascend to the second show level.

On each level, groupers will split their portion of the queue into four groups, to load each of the four theaters. Once directed to their theater, visitors will pick up their 3D glasses before entering a small pre-show room. From there, visitors will walk through a load vestibule before emerging into their theater. It appears that some of the visitors sent to the second show level will ascend to a third show level after they've been assigned their theater and picked up their glasses.

Although this attraction's been compared to Soarin', the load procedure implied by these blueprints better would be compared with Universal's The Simpsons Ride. On Soarin', everyone enters the theaters on one level, to board ride vehicles that then ascend to one of three show levels. On Simpsons and on Avatar, visitors will walk up ramps or steps to their ride level, although the ride vehicles may further elevate from those levels.

Visitors will face curved IMAX-style screens during the show, then will exit through one of two unload vestibules. The plans show visitors on the second and third show levels descending stairs to exit the building, so I presume that all wheelchairs parties will be sent to the first show level to board the attraction. In addition, the two ADA-compatible theaters exit the building at that first show level, while visitors from the two other theaters descend one more floor in their unload vestibule down to an exit corridor that crosses underneath the theater building, so that all four theaters can exit on the same side of the building.

I don't think anyone needs three guesses to figure out that's so all riders can exit into the attraction's gift shop.

What we don't know from these plans are what the ride vehicles will look like, though the plans suggest that they will be suspended from the building's ceiling. Nor, of course, do we know anything about the setting or storyline of the movie itself, beyond what Disney announced at the D23 Expo in Japan — that visitors would fly through the skies of Pandora. However, with four theaters and IMAX-style screens, we do know that this will be one massive show building.

Na'vi River Journey: Late last year at the company's D23 Expo in Japan, Disney revealed details about the boat ride:

"The adventure begins as guests set out in canoes and venture down a mysterious, sacred river hidden within the bioluminescent rainforest. The full beauty of Pandora reveals itself as the canoes pass by exotic glowing plants and amazing creatures. The journey culminates in an encounter with a Na'vi shaman, who has a deep connection to the life force of Pandora and sends positive energy out into the forest through her music."

Rivers of Light: In addition to the new Avatar land, Disney's Animal Kingdom was to open a new night-time show on the park's Discovery River, which surrounded the Tree of Life in the middle of the park. The show initially was scheduled to open in May 2016, but it missed that deadline and still had yet to debut at press time. Rivers of Light steps away from Disney's recent creative trend in theme parks by not being tied to any specific company IP. Instead, it was to offer an original story that evokes tribal legends and classic myth. The show follows four "Animal Spirit Guides" — an elephant, owl, a tiger, and a turtle — whose spiritual journeys frame the production, which will feature water screens, physical props, and lighting effects.

Rivers of Light was expected to open sometime in late 2016 to early 2017.

Other notable attractions scheduled to debut in 2017 include:

Guardians of the Galaxy Mission Breakout at Disney's California Adventure: Disney is replacing The Twilight Zone theme for the park's Tower of Terror drop ride with the narrative from the Tokyo DisneySea version, swapping Taneleer Tivan for Harrison Hightower and bringing the popular Marvel franchise to a Disney theme park attraction for the first time.

Iron Man Experience at Hong Kong Disneyland: Utilizing a Star Tours-type motion simulator, Iron Man Experience will take riders on a flight around Hong Kong, as their trip to the Stark Expo is interrupted by Hydra attempting to steal the world's largest arc reactor.

Symbolica: Palace of Fantasy at Efteling: Visitors collectively will choose one of three different routes within the palace, each offering unique adventures and interactive elements, in this US$38 million attraction — the Dutch theme park's fourth major dark ride.

Project V at Europa Park: Billed as Europe's largest flying theater, Project V (yes, that's a working title) will take visitors on a Soarin'-style journey to some of Europe's most popular tourist destinations. The most expensive individual attraction in the history of Europa Park, the attraction will accommodate 1,400 visitors per hour in two theaters, each with 21 meter screens.

Nemo and Friends SeaRider at Tokyo DisneySea: Replacing the StormRider show and planned for May 12, 2017 debut, this show will follow the characters of "Finding Nemo" and "Finding Dory" on an undersea adventure.

Race Through New York Starring Jimmy Fallon at Universal

Studios Florida: The heart of the new Tonight Show-themed attraction will be a flying theater ride that allows visitors to "race" the Tonight Show host through the streets of New York. The film will include sights of popular New York icons such as the Statue of Liberty and the Empire State Building, as well as cameos from Tonight Show announcer Steve Higgins and band The Roots.

Despicable Me Minion Mayhem at Universal Studios Japan: Minion Park will open in the first half of 2017, as a plussed version of the Minion-themed mini-land at Universal Studios Hollywood. Despicable Me Minion Mayhem will anchor the new land, which Universal is promising will be "the world's largest Minion-themed area."

Submarine Quest at SeaWorld San Diego: This sub-styled track ride will run through outdoor and indoor scenes, including past aquariums holding crabs, eels, octopuses and other marine animals. On board, the subs will feature game-like elements that allow riders to solve tasks they learn about animals depicted in the exhibits.

InvadR at Busch Gardens Williamsburg: InvadR will be a Great Coasters International wooden roller coaster featuring a 74-foot drop, nine airtime hills and a top speed of 48 miles per hour.

Mystic Timbers at Kings Island: Also by Great Coasters International, Mystic Timbers will be 3,265 feet in length, reach 109 feet in height and weave through the park's forested terrain at speeds up to 53 mph.

Ninjago The Ride at Legoland Florida: First installed in California in 2016, this interactive dark ride challenges visitors to train to become ninjas by learning "Spinjitzu." Instead of using a controller to shoot at targets, on Ninjago, you use your hands like a ninja — to launch a variety of blasts at your enemies.

Ferrari Land at PortAventura: Phase one of this new Ferrari-themed land at the Spanish resort will feature an Intamin Vertical Accelerator coaster, with a maximum launch speed of 112 mph.

Justice League Battle for Metropolis at Six Flags Great Adventure and Six Flags Magic Mountain: Winner of the 2015 Theme Park Insider Award for Best New Attraction when in debuted at Six Flags Over Texas, Justice League Battle for Metropolis challenges riders to join Batman, Superman, and other Justice League heroes to fight The Joker, Lex Luthor, and their armies in a battle for control of the city, all while trying to escape The Joker's toxic laughing gas. The ride and its queue feature two animatronic characters in addition to multiple 3D screens and practical effects. The game takes place on 3D and fog screens, with a 360-degree virtual loop thrown in just for kicks.

Volcano Bay at Universal Orlando Resort: Universal was to close its Wet 'n Wild water park — the world's first water park — in 2016, to replace it with this new, more richly themed water park, located on 28 acres next to the Cabana Bay Beach Resort hotel.

Volcano Bay will offer 19 water-based attractions across four themed zones: Rainforest Village, River Village, Wave Village, and Krakatau.

The Krakatau Aqua Coaster will occupy the park's iconic central volcano. The first of its kind in Florida, the coaster will use LIM technology to launch riders upward into the volcano's interior. Visitors will ride in four-person "canoes" through a variety of themed scenes, including tunnels, caves, and past waterfalls.

Krakatau also will feature three drop-floor body slides, including the 125-foot, 70-degree Ko'okiri Body Plunge, "the world's first slide to travel through a pool filled with guests." The volcano also will be home to Punga Racers, "a high-speed race through four different enclosed slides featuring manta-shaped mats."

Other lands will include wave pools, leisure pools, lazy rivers, playgrounds, and raft rides. And no one will have to wait in a line to ride. Universal has announced that all Volcano Bay visitors will get "TapuTapu" wearables that they will use to reserve their places in the park's virtual queues. The wearable will alert visitors when it is their turn to ride.

Visitors also will be able tap the TapuTapu wearable (get the name, now?) to activate "tap to play" experiences through the park, including water cannons and special effects inside the volcano. In a Universal Orlando promo video, we see that TapuTapu is kinda of an Apple Watch meets MagicBand, a waterproof wristband that seems to include a display screen, presumably to let you know when to return to a ride.

Volcano Bay is scheduled to open by summer of 2017.

Not included on this list: Disney's highly anticipated **Star Wars Land**, which is now under construction at Disneyland in California and Disney's Hollywood Studios at Walt Disney World in Florida.

In California, drivers approaching the Mickey and Friends parking structure via the flyover from the Interstate 5 exit have the best view of the site, which offers an unobstructed view of the cleared land all the way back to Big Thunder Mountain. Disney has closed the Rivers of America and is creating a new course for the northern half of that waterway, to create more land north of Frontierland for the Star Wars project.

In Florida, Walt Disney World closed the Streets of America and the Lights, Motors, Action stunt show in Hollywood Studios, clearing the way for the start of construction on the east-coast version of Star Wars Land.

On each coast, Star Wars Land will feature two major attractions: one where riders will fly the Millennium Falcon and another where they will be caught in a battle with the villainous First Order. The land also will include Cantina dining, character meet and greets, abundant retail, and role-playing cast members, creating the experience of visiting a new planet in the Star Wars universe.

At 14 acres each, the Star Wars Land projects will be the largest themed lands Disney's history when they are completed. When will that be? Disney hasn't said yet, but Insiders are projecting that the lands will open sometime in 2019 or 2020, with the Disneyland version appearing on track to open first.

Disney also is working on a **Toy Story Land** for Disney's Hollywood Studios, occupying the space where Catastrophe Canyon, the boneyard, and costume shop used to stand.

The idea is that we are in Andy's backyard — and we have been reduced to the size of a toy so we can play with the other toys on some of the contraptions that Andy has built.

On the Slinky Dog Dash roller coaster, we are riding on a track that Andy has built with his "Mega Coaster Play Kit," riding on the back of Slinky Dog, whom Andy has put on the track to test his stretching limits. Alien Swirling Saucers is a playset of Andy's where visitors will ride on spinning flying saucers, controlled by the Little Green Men, as "The Claw" looms above them, ready to strike.

Universal Orlando also is building **Fast & Furious - Supercharged** for a 2018 debut. A plussed version of the Studio Tour encounter of the same name at Universal Studios Hollywood, the attraction will walk visitors through a garage filled with show cars from the popular Fast & Furious series before they board trams for a simulated high-speed chase through the streets of Los Angeles. Fast & Furious - Supercharged replaces the old Disaster! attraction in the park.

Beyond 2018, Universal's next big announced project is **Nintendo**, for which the company has secured the in-park attraction rights. Universal has not announced any specific rides or attractions for its Nintendo project, or even which parks will host the new land.

Founded in Japan in the late nineteenth century as a playing card company, Nintendo got into the video game business in the 1970s. Its franchises include Pokemon, Mario Bros., The Legend of Zelda, and Donkey Kong. Creators of the Wii console, Nintendo today trails Sony and Microsoft in sales of home console units, but its games are considered to skew more family friendly than the first-person shooter games more popular on PlayStation and XBox.

The deal with Universal allows the two companies to develop three-dimensional, interactive experiences in theme park settings that recreate and potentially advance the characters, settings, situations and narratives made popular in Nintendo's games.

Please read us online at www.themeparkinsider.com for coverage and reviews of all these new attractions as they approach their official openings.

Thank you for joining us for this look back at 2016!

ABOUT THE AUTHOR

Robert Niles is the founder and editor of ThemeParkInsider.com, an online consumers' guide to the world's leading theme and amusement parks, read by more than 300,000 people each month. It has been named the top theme park site on the Internet by Forbes and Travel + Leisure magazines, has been a Webby Award finalist, and is a winner of the prestigious Online Journalism Award, then presented by the Online News Association and the Columbia Graduate School of Journalism. In addition to writing for and editing Theme Park Insider, Robert also writes a weekly column on theme parks for the Orange County Register.

Robert worked at Walt Disney World's Magic Kingdom for five summers between 1987 and 1991, as well as for a full year between graduating Northwestern University and beginning graduate school in journalism at another university. In the years since leaving Disney, Robert's worked as a reporter, editorial writer, columnist, and website editor for several newspapers, including The [Bloomington, Indiana] Herald-Times, the Omaha [Nebraska] World-Herald, the [Denver] Rocky Mountain News and the Los Angeles Times.

You can follow ThemeParkInsider.com on the Internet at http://www.themeparkinsider.com

We're also on Facebook at http://www.facebook.com/themeparkinsider

And Twitter at http://twitter.com/themepark